ART DECO
HOUSE STYLE

ART DECO
HOUSE STYLE

AN ARCHITECTURAL AND INTERIOR DESIGN SOURCE BOOK

INGRID CRANFIELD

David & Charles

Copyright © Megra Mitchell 2001
Text copyright © Ingrid Cranfield 2001

Conceived by John Strange & Megra Mitchell

Designed by Megra Mitchell

First published 2001

A catalogue record for this book is available
from the British Library

ISBN 0 7153 0964 1

Printed in Italy by Milanostampa s.p.a.
for David & Charles
Brunel House   Newton Abbot   Devon   TQ12 4PU

Please note that much of the photographic and design material in this book is from
vintage sources and may not be as clear as contemporary reproductions.

CONTENTS

Introduction

Art Deco architecture was an architecture of ornament, geometry, energy, retrospection, optimism, colour, texture, light, and at times even symbolism.

Patricia Bayer

What will today's art and architecture be called in fifty or a hundred years' time? Which of its characteristics will be regarded as typical or defining? And to what socio-economic and political circumstances will its origin be attributed?

Half a century elapsed between the heyday of Art Deco and the application to it of that name. Art Deco artists and designers did not so designate themselves. Nor, indeed, were they such a homogeneous bunch that they would have recognized a unity among themselves. They were reacting in similar ways to contemporary moods and mores, responding to common stimuli, enjoying the same kind of access to materials and producing items that bore some resemblance to each other. If this seems a broad and vague characterization, that is because Art Deco artists were freer to express their individuality through choice of styles, materials and techniques than any artists hitherto.

The birth of 'Art Deco'

Art Deco originally developed in France between the years 1908 and 1912, then overflowed into every Western country and reached a high point from 1925 to 1935. The term derives from the Exposition Internationale des Arts Décoratifs et Industriels Modernes held in Paris in 1925. In 1966, that exhibition was revived at the Musée des Arts Décoratifs in Paris, and it was then that the term 'Art Deco' was coined. Since then, it has been applied to a wide variety of works produced between the two world wars, even to those from other recognized schools of design, such as the German Bauhaus.

OPPOSITE: *A modern version of an Art Deco glass design for a window or lamp.*

ABOVE: *A design produced by* pochoir, *a stencilling technique popular in France during the Art Deco period. Vibrant colours intensify the impact of the design.*

Kansacraft

Originally planned for 1908, the Exposition was postponed a number of times, partly because of the outbreak of World War I. Unlike the Expositions Universelles that had preceded it, this was a project sponsored by the French government with the specific aim of developing export markets for French decorative and applied arts. It was also an attempt to solve the problems that had been caused by the introduction of the machine into the artistic process. These included the division of labour between artists, craftsmen and commercial manufacturers and increasing competition from abroad in the trade in luxury goods, in which France had hitherto been a leader. Other concerns were the professional training of artisans and legislation on apprenticeship. At the beginning of the twentieth century, Paris had more artisans than any other European city. It was not only their survival that was at stake, however, but also French national prestige, to which the production and quality of luxury crafts had been essential contributors.

When the Exposition eventually took place, between April and October 1925, more than twenty nations participated. Notable exceptions were Germany – a significant omission because it was there that the Bauhaus school had developed – and the USA, whose secretary of commerce, Herbert Hoover, felt that it could not meet the requirements for entry in terms of modernity or originality. Instead, a 108-member US delegation, composed of trade organizations and art guilds, was sent to Paris to glean ideas with a view to encouraging American industry to take a lead in design innovation. Britain participated rather half-heartedly, having mounted its own British Empire Exhibition in the previous year. Furniture by Gordon Russell and Ambrose Heal formed cornerstones of the British exhibit in Paris.

The Exposition, occupying a huge area in central Paris, included over 130 exhibits mounted by artistic, commercial and industrial establishments, as well as hundreds more exhibits by individual artists. The pavilions at the

OPPOSITE: *A medley of architectural notions depicted in stained glass for the 1925 Paris Exposition.*

THIS PAGE: *A selection of stained-glass panels on display at the 1925 Exposition in Paris.*

Exposition that attracted most attention, both at the time and subsequently, were built in a style that is now associated with Art Deco. The most popular of the French pavilions were devoted to a specific theme in which a number of artists collaborated. Among them was the sumptuous 'Hôtel d'un Collectionneur' presented by Emile-Jacques Ruhlmann, with architecture by Pierre Patout, furniture by Ruhlmann, lacquerwork by Jean Dunand, forged ironwork by Edgar Brandt, sculpture by Joseph-Antoine Bernard, François Pompon and Emile-Antoine Bourdelle and even a large decorative painting, *Les Perruches* (*The Parrots*), by Jean Dupas, one of the few painters whose work could justly be termed 'Art Deco'.

The major department stores in Paris had their own pavilions – Au Printemps (Primavera), Galeries Lafayette (La Maîtrise), Au Bon Marché (La Pomone) and the Grands Magasins du Louvre (Studium). The Swiss architect Le Corbusier designed one pavilion, naming it L'Esprit Nouveau. It was a model of Modernism, with plain white walls, a concrete frame and large expanses of glass, all unified by a rigid geometry. The interior was fitted out with unpretentious furniture of a kind that was already commercially available, such as classic bentwood chairs designed by Michael Thonet (1796–1871), which had been in production since 1853.

The Exposition programme stipulated that everything included had to be 'modern' (achieving 'the maximum of novelty and the minimum of traditional influence') and that objects displayed should be in keeping with the tenet that form must follow function. If these were the principles, then it might seem that the aim of the exhibition was to enhance co-operation between art and industry. Yet there was another goal, which conflicted with this idea: the preservation of traditional craftsmanship and skills that were otherwise doomed to disappear, by finding modern applications for their products. These traditional handicrafts were not the work of quaint, folksy outfits: they were produced by studios that pursued high-art, elaborate workmanship, turning out finely crafted individual or limited-edition pieces for an exclusive market.

Later, Modernist architecture and design put paid to such elitism and idealism. The Modernists believed that excellence in design should be accessible to all and that mass production was not inconsistent with high quality.

Artistic sources of Art Deco

Art Deco – or the *style moderne* as it was then called – had begun evolving around the turn of the twentieth century and many of its constituent elements were in place before 1914. Formally, it both grew out of, and was a reaction to,

However, there were many other sources of inspiration for Art Deco, including Cubism, the Bauhaus, the Ballets Russes, the Glasgow School of Art under Charles Rennie Mackintosh, the Vienna Secession, the Deutsche Werkbund, Russian Constructivism and the Dutch De Stijl movement. The arts of ancient Egypt, Africa, the Americas and the East also inspired Western artists and designers. The discovery in 1922 of Tutankhamun's tomb helped to make Egyptian art familiar and popular.

Cubist painting had the most universal influence on Art Deco because of the way it explored the geometric qualities of its subjects, its treatment of planes and its use of colour. Pablo Picasso and George Braque, its leading exponents, had a strong impact on contemporary designers.

The Bauhaus was a German school of architecture and design, formed in 1919 under the leadership of Walter Gropius. Its designers were among the first to propose that the forms of objects should be determined by their purpose, materials and manufacture. Ornament, which was necessarily derived from older styles, compromised purity of design. Luxuries were held to be socially irresponsible. In its early days, Art Deco was characterized by ornament and luxury, but the principles of austerity and simplicity began to make their mark when Bauhaus designers, fleeing persecution in Germany after 1933, went to the USA and influenced the American Art Deco movement.

An early inspiration for Art Deco design was the sets and costumes of Diaghilev's Ballets Russes, which took Paris by storm when it made its début in 1909. This explosion of vibrant colour and exoticism – in particular the stupendous designs of Léon Bakst – sounded the death knell for the pale, delicate motifs of Art Nouveau, which now gave way to bold lines and geometric blocks of colour.

The work of Charles Rennie Mackintosh (1868–1928) at the Glasgow School of Art typified the so-called 'severe' side of Art Nouveau, which eschewed the exuberance and curvilinearity of its baroque mode. His designs featured parallel lines, flat shapes and greatly elongated, stylized, semi-abstract figures. Mackintosh's style had a profound impact on the young Viennese artists who, in 1897, formed the group known as the Vienna Secession in protest at the conservatism of the Vienna Academy. Their style was elegant, refined and functional, with a penchant for squares and rectangles. In the same city were the Wiener Werkstätte – furniture workshops which created cosmopolitan designs of striking originality. Here, for the first time, the concept of total design was put into full effect. The entire environment, from the structure of a building to its domestic furnishings and ornaments, even to clothing and jewellery, was regarded as a total work of art.

the French Art Nouveau style. Both deployed a decorative repertoire based on nature but, whereas Art Nouveau often featured exotic flowers and plants with twisting and climbing stems in running motifs, usually integrated into the structure of an object, Art Deco was much more restrained, preferring stylized and geometricized flowers – often roses – in bouquets or baskets. The French decorator Paul Follot created what is deemed to be one of the first Art Deco works, a dining-room ensemble in sycamore, ebony and amaranth, which was exhibited at the Salon d'Automne of 1912 (now in the Musée des Arts Décoratifs, Paris). The chair backs were fashioned in an openwork design representing a basket of fruit and flowers.

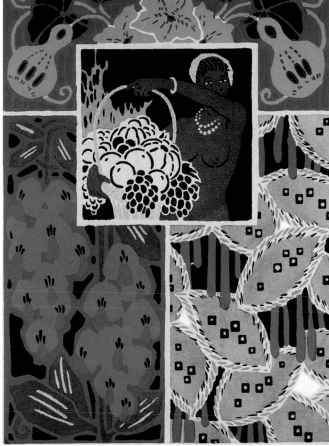

Opposite: *An extravagant geometrical design characterizes this beautiful tapestry (1927-28) by Gunta Stadler-Stölzl, a pupil and later instructor at the Bauhaus in Dessau.*

This page: *A selection of pochoir (stencilled) designs from the Art Deco period, showing ancient Egyptian and African influences.*

The couturier Paul Poiret (1879–1944) and the architect and decorator Louis Süe (1875–1968) both visited the Wiener Werkstätte. On their return to Paris, Poiret founded the Ecole d'Art Décoratif Martine and Atelier Martine in 1911. Poiret's designs reached a wide audience, notably through the illustrations of Paul Iribe (1883–1935) and Georges Lepape (1887–1971). Süe founded the Atelier Français in Paris in 1912 and aimed at a modern style that nevertheless retained links with French tradition.

The Deutsche Werkbund ('design association'), itself influenced by the British Arts and Crafts movement, had promoted links between art, architecture and industry since 1907, and emphasized functional design that was suitable for mass-produced goods but also aesthetically pleasing. Ornament had only secondary importance.

Constructivism evolved as the favoured style in Russia after the Revolution of 1917. It was based on the belief that art has a social purpose and should be put to the service of the state. Works in this genre consisted of geometric forms that looked like machinery and used lettering in new ways, which later turned up in Art Deco graphic work.

RIGHT: *Design by Henri Sauvage for an apartment complex to be built on the banks of the Seine in Paris.*

BELOW: *Bas-reliefs from the Pavilion of Tourism at the 1925 Paris Exposition, which was designed by Robert Mallet-Stevens.*

The style of the Dutch De Stijl movement was simple and striking: rectangles of colour separated by dark grid lines made such works distinctive and recognizable. Although De Stijl artists were excluded from the Paris Exposition in 1925, their style made a clear impact on one of its most striking structures, the Pavilion of Tourism, designed by the French Modernist Robert Mallet-Stevens. This building, comprising intersecting and layered slabs of reinforced concrete, exemplified the International style.

Other buildings at the exhibition, however, had a greater impact on the future public face of Art Deco architecture, featuring neoclassical columns, stepped masses, monumental entrances and stylized decoration. All these ideas, and the movements from which they derived, mingled and became modified to form Art Deco.

Social antecedents

We have looked at the artistic origins of Art Deco, but where, in a deeper sense, did it come from? Art Deco was a response to the conditions and preoccupations of the time, beginning with the devastation and hardship caused by World War I. The keynotes of the era were optimism and escapism – optimism because that war was characterized as 'the war to end all wars'; escapism because reality was, for most people, harsh and uncertain.

In a book entitled *Contempo: This American Tempo*, published in 1929, Ruth and John Vassos reflected the preoccupations of the era – a love affair with machines, a delight in speed, particularly in the form of the subway, an admiration for 'the great god RADIO' and a profound cynicism, not to mention an unpleasant anti-Semitism (of which the worst was yet to come).

Art Deco was all about escapism: its works, especially its graphic art, represented the fantasy world portrayed in Hollywood musicals – an unattainable world of sophistication, exuberance and of carefree, fast, moneyed living. The so-called Odeon Style, executed in chromium, coloured glass and painted concrete and applied to the many Odeon cinemas that opened during the 1930s in Britain and the USA, was a means of creating opulence at a relatively low price. It provided a world of apparent lavish glamour as a counterbalance to the hardship of the decade that experienced the Great Depression. This manifestation of the Art Deco style popularized it and made it acceptable in domestic objects, especially those that represented modernity, such as radios.

General characteristics of Art Deco style

Geometric forms; zigzags, sunbursts and chevrons in abstract patterns and rendered in brilliant colours; the use of bronze, ebony, ivory and exotic woods: all these are now recognized as principal distinguishing features of Art Deco style. However, designers of the interwar years could be divided into two broad categories: those who rejoiced in decoration and would happily cover every available surface with flowers and fruit, fountains and leaping gazelles; and those who rejected decoration in favour of pure form, turning for inspiration to the aesthetics of machinery.

The latter group revolved around avant-garde schools of architecture and their leaders, most notably the Swiss-born Le Corbusier, who famously opined that a house should be 'a machine for living in'. Criticized in its early days for its opulence, Art Deco soon came down to earth and ceased to be the preserve of the wealthy. New, inexpensive materials such as Bakelite came into copious use. In architecture, coloured glass and chromium-plated steel were used to create the Art Deco look at little cost. Blocks of flats were often decorated with Art Deco motifs, especially around the roofs, entrances, lobbies and window surrounds. Parallel horizontal lines were popular decorations for exterior walls, often grouped into threes and sometimes 'pulvinated' (swelling out from the flat surface). Flattened columns were another common feature, as were coloured glass inserts and, for interiors, moulded plaster painted in geometric designs.

The concept of total design, pioneered in the Wiener Werkstätte, became one of the supreme tenets of Art Deco and was adhered to by artists of both categories. Every detail of a decorative scheme – from keyholes to kitchens, rugs to radiators, taps to tiles – was dignified by the designer's attention. The recipients of such complete schemes were more often industrial buildings than private homes. As a result, few survive in their entirety. Most were destroyed or diminished as industry responded to technological advance with reconstructions, renovations and changes of usage.

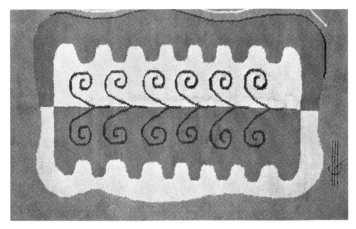

TOP: *A rug designed by Ronald Grierson and produced by the Redfern Publishing Co., mid-1930s.*

ABOVE: *Balustrade at the Paramount Theatre, Paris. The architects were Auguste Bluysen and J. P. Mangeaut and the ironwork was designed by Raymond Subes.*

LEFT: *An interior door by Edgar Brandt, renowned as an ironwork designer.*

For a summary of the general principles of Art Deco, we could do worse than turn to an article by James Laver in the July 1933 issue of *Design for To-day* on the great exhibitions of the past and the styles they promoted. Laver berated Art Nouveau as having 'produced some of the worst horrors in the whole history of furnishing', including items of supreme impracticality – describing it as 'a courageous march into the blindest of blind alleys'. He went on:

When, twenty-five years later, another Great Exhibition was opened in Paris, it was quite obvious that the style of 1900 [Art Nouveau] had been swept away and forgotten. Sufficient time has passed for us to see the Exposition des Arts Décoratifs…in some kind of historical perspective, and it must be admitted that some of its exhibits look curiously old-fashioned already. But the principles which underlay

the best of them are still valid to-day, and have had an enormous influence all over the world. These principles were: a striving after simplicity; the use of materials in accordance with their natural properties; a new care for hygiene in the designing of windows and in the suppression of dust-catching fabrics; diffused lighting made possible by electrical improvements; the use of modern methods of heating and refrigeration; and a general tendency to prefer use to decoration. All these tendencies were reinforced by the smallness of most modern dwellings, from which drawing rooms full of knick-knacks have disappeared, their place taken by a living room which, like the mediaeval hall, is often a dining room as well. If some of the exhibits of 1925 are already out of date, it is because progress has been steady along the lines which they suggested, and when the next Great Exhibition comes to be held – there is one in Chicago this very year – the same principles will be still in evidence, although the extreme simplicity of the early "functional" epoch may be found to have been somewhat modified and softened by a new decorative style.

Characteristics of French Art Deco style

Many of the characteristics of what was to become the Art Deco style were identified in a manifesto by André Vera, a French landscape artist and garden theorist, published in January 1912 in *L'Art décoratif* under the title 'Le Nouveau Style'. Vera contended that a modern style of decorative arts should continue French traditions, while rejecting both internationalism and pastiche. For decoration he advocated contrasts of rich, bold colours and baskets or garlands of flowers in place of the eighteenth-century French repertoire of torches and bows and arrows. This traditional current was reinforced after World War I by the notion of a *retour à l'ordre* ('return to order'), made manifest by references to French classical art, especially in decorative painting, sculpture and ceramics.

The Art Deco movement in France was led by Louis Süe and the decorator André Mare, founders in 1919 of the Compagnie des Arts Français, their colleagues André Groult, Clément Mère and Paul Follot, and the master cabinetmaker Emile-Jacques Ruhlmann. They continued to work in the traditions of French *ébénisterie* (fine carpentry), using unusual combinations of luxurious and exotic materials, especially from Africa and Asia, such as ebony, palmwood, rosewood and shagreen (the rough skin of the spotted dogfish). Distinctive features of their work were contrasts of textures, colours and materials and

OPPOSITE: *A small commode of mahogany and sharkskin, with inlaid and carved ebony, by Paul Iribe.*

BELOW: *A mahogany armchair and round table with a single ebony support, from the workshops of the Compagnie des Arts Français, 1925. On the table is a faïence pipe-vase.*

BELOW: *Chest of drawers by Emile-Jacques Ruhlmann, 1924. It is decorated in macassar ebony veneer and ivory.*

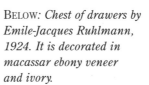

complicated techniques such as lacquerwork, marquetry and pieces inlaid with ivory or mother-of-pearl. They often incorporated ingenious devices into furnishings, such as desktops that swivelled or inclined, or flaps that folded down. This penchant for multipurpose pieces of furniture persisted throughout the Art Deco period, though the Compagnie des Arts Français dispersed in 1928.

The Parisian firm of Saddier produced some of the best items of this kind in the 1920s and 1930s. For example, a dressing table was combined with a stool or incorporated a huge circular mirror with low shelves on either side. In some cases, light fittings – usually vertical neon tubes set into chromium fittings – were part of the design. These pieces were practical and attractive and reflected the feeling of the later Art Deco era that furniture did not need to be formal and could be treated in a light-hearted, even jokey way. Another feature of Art Deco furniture of the 1920s was that the entire surface tended to be decorated, perhaps with a picture, as was common in Japanese art.

A stylized rose, designed by Paul Iribe and nicknamed the *'rose Iribe',* was a particularly potent symbol of Art

Deco, even of the spirit of France at that time. Along with conventionalized marguerites, dahlias and zinnias, pomegranates, swags of drapery with ropes of pearls, ribbons, doves, deer and fountains, it reappeared constantly in building designs. In furniture and interior design, the oval was a favourite shape. In ironwork, the spiral was a recurring motif. Angular forms, the use of bright materials such as stainless steel and mirror glass, and a fondness for certain non-traditional decorative motifs were the other main characteristics of French Art Deco.

France continued to lead in every field of decorative art, even after World War I, when shortages of materials and labour were to some extent offset by the removal of the threat of competition from Germany. The status of French design was a matter of national pride and prestige. In addition, the export of luxury goods brought in vast amounts of money and was indeed the cornerstone of the French economy. Buyers from all parts of the world flocked to Paris, and French designers and artists remained the arbiters of international taste and fashion.

The decline of a luxury style

Whereas in France Art Deco manifested itself in an exuberant, ornamental guise, in the rest of Europe and the USA in the 1920s it took the form of spare, simple design. The latter may be termed 'Modernism' to distinguish it from the French style, which is the essential Art Deco. Both strains were sometimes known as 'Moderne', especially in America, where the term 'Jazz Moderne' is also sometimes used to denote Art Deco.

The production of luxury goods clashed with the concept of Modernism. Modernists championed fitness for purpose, and though this was also one of the tenets of Art Deco, its exponents were happy to combine function with ornamentation. The architect Serge Chermayeff, speaking to a branch of the Society of Industrial Artists in 1932, made it clear that his preferences lay with the Modernist style. He advocated functionality, simplicity, the avoidance of ornament and the necessity for integrating design into the essence of the product.

Design critics and manufacturers clung to different ideals. Commentators tended to regard commercial success as artistic failure, while manufacturers believed that adopting the latest simple modern designs would bring them commercial failure. Artists understood neither the new materials nor the preoccupations of manufacturers, while quality and sales volume were the top priorities of the manufacturers.

Other factors contributed to the decline of ornament in design: the increasing intrusion of machines into people's lives; the emergence, especially from the Bauhaus, of new and revolutionary steel furniture; in fashion, the greater activity and participation of women in public life, which necessitated simpler, freer clothing. Gradually the elegant refinement of Art Deco, with its gracious curves and flower ornament, gave way to angular, unadorned surfaces. Throughout the 1920s and 1930s, the 'modern' and the 'Modernist' developed together, often colliding and causing friction. The modern was, simply, an expression of good design, whereas the Modernist was a form of chic that was hard and uncompromising.

In his introduction to the *Design Industries Association Yearbook* for 1924–25, John Gloag pleaded for realistic caution in the pursuit of Modernism. Nikolaus Pevsner, in *An Enquiry into Industrial Art in England* (1937), recognized that life itself is not ordered or efficient and that achieving order and efficiency in design is an unrealizable dream. He held the 'ominous Paris Exhibition of 1925' responsible for the introduction of 'bad "Modernism" into the trade'. 'Modernism' in its 'jazz forms', he contended, had 'spoiled the market for serious modern work'. Pevsner questioned the assumption that 'nothing of vital energy and beauty can be created unless it be fit for its purpose, clear, straightforward and simple'.

The 1925 Exposition marked both the summit and the beginning of the demise of Art Deco, most noticeably in France, as a more functionalist and internationalist group of designers emerged who were opposed to the decorative extravagance, nationalism and traditionalism of Art Deco. In France these designers formed the Union des Artistes Modernes in 1929. It could be argued that the influence of Art Deco continued in France during the 1930s in such ensembles as the liner *Normandie* (1935), but by 1930 proportions were becoming more monumental and forms heavier and fuller, without the ornamental exuberance so characteristic of Art Deco in its original sense.

the suburbs inevitably meant that the new buildings included certain Art Deco elements. Few houses were ever built that were pure Art Deco from top to bottom – and even fewer people nowadays have the luck to live in such houses.

For this reason, this book has not confined itself strictly to 'Art Deco house style' but deals more generally with the domestic style and decoration of the interwar years.

Art Deco in the USA

The Paris Exposition of 1925 had been immensely popular and spawned lavish government-sponsored publications featuring the works displayed in the French section. As a result, the Art Deco style became widely diffused, especially in the USA, where it was further popularized by the look and image of Hollywood films. In the USA, the term 'Moderne' was used to describe a style that was somewhere between Art Deco and an expression of the Modernist movement. Moderne buildings made heavy use of chromium

OPPOSITE AND ABOVE: *The Midland Hotel, Morecambe. Designed by Oliver Hill, the plan of the entire building conforms to the curve of the coast. The south wall of the hall (opposite) was decorated with a stone panel carved in flat relief by Eric Gill, and the impressive circular staircase has hand-rails of polished aluminum and treads inlaid with blue rubber.*

RIGHT: *The Coca-Cola Company Bottling Plant in Los Angeles was designed in 1936 in the form of a steamship by Robert V. Derrah, to reflect the chairman's interest in ships.*

BELOW RIGHT: *The Niagara Mohawk Power Corporation Building in West Syracuse, New York. Architects Bley & Leyman, 1930–32.*

The beginnings of a mass style

It was during the interwar years that a new phenomenon evolved throughout the United Kingdom, North America, Australia and New Zealand and parts of Europe: the rise of suburbia. Growing industrialization led to the movement of large numbers of people away from rural areas to find employment in cities; the democratization of the motor car and the extension of public transport networks – not least the new underground rail systems – also played their part. The gaps that had once separated towns and cities from their outlying villages were filled in, creating large zoned conurbations. Most of the buildings that were erected in these urban outer rings were domestic housing of an affordable kind.

These houses were not of course exclusively or even principally Art Deco creations. Art Deco was an exceptionally pervasive style, influencing most aspects of people's lives, but it was primarily a style of surface decoration. Nevertheless, the coincidence between Art Deco's flowering and the growth of

and other new materials, but were not stripped of all ornament, as were the later Modernist structures.

The Metropolitan Museum of Art in New York made a number of purchases from the Paris Exposition, while a display of 400 objects travelled to major American cities in 1926 and the department store Lord & Taylor held an exhibition of Moderne style in 1928. However, during the period from 1925–35, little was actually produced in the USA to which the term 'Art Deco' could be aptly applied. The USA did not have the tradition of luxury craftsmanship that had blossomed into Art Deco in France. The style was, however, adapted when it crossed the Atlantic. Kenneth Frampton wrote in *Modern Architecture*:

From the American point of view, the First World War had been favourably concluded; America had emerged a creditor nation and the boom of the 1920s was about to start. In what style could such an enthusiasm for 'progress' be expressed? Certainly not in the historicist styles of waning European power – nor for that matter could it adopt the avant-garde mode of the new Europe…Its sources had to be more open and eclectic.

Many talented European designers emigrated to the USA, fleeing the persecutions and aggressions that were to precipitate World War II. They took with them their ideas

OPPOSITE: *This suburban station on the Pennsylvania Railroad represents many of the features of Art Deco style, notably geometrical symmetry.*

THIS PAGE: *The Empire State Building (right) and the Chrysler Building (far right), in New York City, typified the pyramid-like shape of skyscrapers. The Chrysler Building has some notable Art Deco interior features.*

and skills, thus stirring America into a new era of innovation in architecture and the decorative arts. They included the industrial designers Joseph Urban, Paul Frankl and Kem Weber from Vienna, who worked in a rational, geometric style that had emerged largely from the Wiener Werkstätte, rather than from the French *style moderne*. Frankl drew on the Viennese style and the austere simplicity of modern American architecture to make his famous 'Skyscraper' bookcase in about 1928. Other designers in America combined the polychrome decoration and geometric shapes of Moderne style with the machine aesthetic, thus taking Art Deco forward by imbuing it with urban sophistication and rationalism and applying to it a modern use of materials.

The Radio City Music Hall in New York City opened in December 1932, its exterior decorated with three circular plaques of metal and enamel showing allegorical reliefs of the figures of song, dance and drama. The aim of the architects (Edward Durrell as design architect, Donald Deskey as interior design co-ordinator), stated in the publicity handout, was 'to achieve a complete decorative scheme that is an example of sane modern design, as differentiated from modernistic design that merely takes as a starting point deviation from an established form'. A jazz motif throughout this building illustrates why Art Deco was sometimes equated with 'Jazz' style. Like many other buildings of the time, this 'sane modern design' was born out of a conglomeration of ideas including Aztec and Egyptian art, the Ballets Russes and all the other artistic predecessors of Art Deco. Even the architect may not have known precisely what inspired him.

Much has been written about the origin of the pyramid-like shape of skyscrapers. In fact, the reason for this shape was essentially mundane. The zoning laws of 1916, intended to prevent overcrowding and to permit the entry of as much light and air as possible, forbade the construction of towers that rose in a solid mass. The greater its height, the narrower the tower had to be in relation to the total ground space the building occupied.

Another famous New York skyscraper – the Chrysler Building of 1929 by William Van Alen (1883–1954) – displayed Art Deco influence in the decorative stainless-steel sunburst of the upper floors. Inside, the lobby, with its expensive marbles and elevator doors decorated with an intarsia design in the form of a papyrus flower, is also a masterpiece of the style. Ely Jacques Kahn (1884–1972) was responsible for a large number of Art Deco skyscrapers in the 1920s and 1930s. His namesake Albert

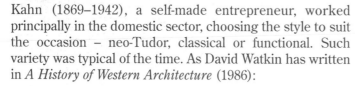

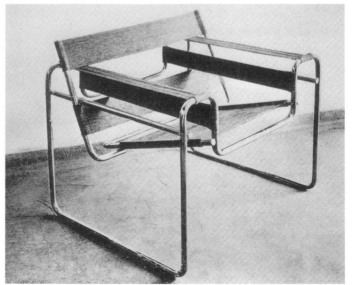

Unquestionably every Englishman who visits the pavilions and stands of the modern French ensembliers will ask himself whether he would care to live among such impeccable surroundings from which cosiness is markedly absent…our Englishman, mindful of fireside joys, of capacious easy chairs, will, perhaps, admire, then turn aside and leave such artificialities to the exhibition and to France.

The new ideas did of course filter through to Britain and find some degree of acceptance, although they appealed only to a minority and were regarded by many as the province of left-wing intellectuals. There was little quintessential Bauhaus design, founded on geometry, to be found in Britain, though modern furniture – square or, later, rounded curves in plain veneer – could be obtained from various sources such as Heal's of London. Gordon Russell began making steel and laminated wood furniture in the early 1930s. Textile designers had greater commercial success in Britain: Edward McKnight Kauffer and Marion Dorn created Cubist abstract designs for rugs and carpets, which were handwoven at the Wilton Carpet Factory from 1928 onwards. In the same year Edinburgh Weavers was established, which also produced textile designs in a modern idiom.

In the 1920s and 1930s, the distinguishable strands in English architecture were the neo-Georgian (a simplified form of classical), modern and – never a dominant style in England – Art Deco. W. M. Dudok (1884–1974) was a Dutch architect who worked in the modern idiom. His influence spread across Europe and was best represented

Kahn (1869–1942), a self-made entrepreneur, worked principally in the domestic sector, choosing the style to suit the occasion – neo-Tudor, classical or functional. Such variety was typical of the time. As David Watkin has written in *A History of Western Architecture* (1986):

in a typically American combination of industrial dynamism and social conservatism, a business tycoon of these years might live in a neo-Tudor suburban mansion, work in an Art Deco skyscraper, visit a neo-Georgian country club at the weekends, and educate his sons at a neo-Gothic college, all built in the 1920s.

Art Deco in Britain

The reaction in Britain to the 1925 Paris Exposition was lukewarm. *The Architectural Review* of that year commented:

in Britain by Thomas Tait (1882–1954). However, the modern style had no impact before 1930 and little until after World War II. Its proponents advocated a return to first principles and concentrated their attentions on mass housing, the location of industry and the growth of towns.

In 1933, having hitherto lagged behind their European counterparts, British architects formed themselves into the Modern Architectural Research Group (MARS), a branch of the Congrès Internationaux d'Architecture Moderne (CIAM, founded in Switzerland in 1928). One of MARS's important achievements was Highpoint Flats, Highgate (1935). Emigrés such as Marcel Breuer, Serge Chermayeff and Walter Gropius stayed in Britain for only a short time before moving on to the USA. but their influence was great. They raised the morale of the British Modernists and helped them to feel part of an international movement, although the lack of patrons for experimental new building frustrated both groups of architects.

OPPOSITE, LEFT: *A room design from the catalogue of the furniture-maker and retailer, Heal's of London.*

OPPOSITE, RIGHT *The famous Wassily chair of tubular steel by Marcel Breuer, 1925.*

THIS PAGE: *Torfyn rug designed and made by Alexander Morton, Sons & Co. (above) and a design by Ronald Grierson (right), produced by the Redfern Publishing Co. Designers of the mid-1930s were concerned to treat a room as a unit, which had to be 'organic'.*

Chapter 1
The Architects, their Ideas & Works

All houses should be white by law. This cleanliness shows objects in their absolute veracity and implies the obligation of absolute purity.

Le Corbusier

Once the buildings of the 1925 Paris Exposition had been pulled down, the ideas and concepts they represented receded to the back of architects' minds. A few commercial buildings being erected at the time acquired new façades in the *style moderne*, but otherwise the new look made little impact on architecture in Europe, even in Paris. Europe had other worries, having just suffered the dreadful destruction of World War I. Recovery was going on, but this was not accompanied by construction on any large scale.

Things were different in America, where a construction boom occurred in the 1920s. There, skyscrapers and other public and commercial buildings were erected, transforming the major cities all across the country, and delighting the world with their height, shapes and decorative schemes. It was in such buildings that American Art Deco was most manifest, as the designers looked to the new style flourishing in Paris for a decorative idiom suitable for such thoroughly modern architecture. One critic described skyscrapers of the period as 'proudly individualistic towers of the nineteen-twenties and thirties, those "cathedrals of commerce" and castles in the sky' (Arthur Lehmann, *The Metropolitan Museum of Art Bulletin*, 1971). Domestic structures were also built in the Art Deco style, but in much smaller numbers. With the stockmarket crash of 1929 and the Great Depression that followed, construction initially fell back, but then revived as a result of government incentives and programmes. The

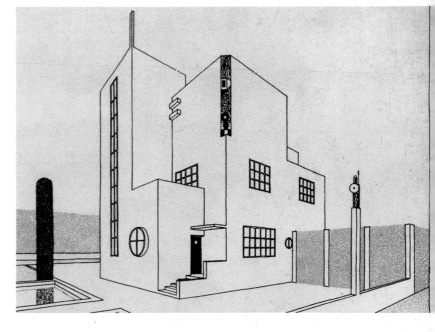

OPPOSITE: *This house in Gidea Park, Essex, was built by Berthold Lubetkin in about 1935 and its image appeared for years on Kellog's cornflake packets as the 'sunshine house', an emblem of modern living. There are large French windows or doors on the* south and west sides. It has a sun terrace, a promenade balcony and piloti columns like those found in Le Corbusier houses.*

ABOVE: *A pen-and-ink drawing by Robert Mallet-Stevens of a design for a villa, 1923.*

LEFT: *Folding screen of wrought iron highlighted with gold, entitled 'The Oasis'. It was designed by Edgar Brandt for the 1925 Paris Exposition.*

OPPOSITE: *Foyer of the Martel House, Paris, designed by Robert Mallet-Stevens. The multi-faceted mirror was by Joël and Jan Martel.*

Work Projects Administration supported the construction of many Art Deco projects and several fairs and expositions were built in the Art Deco style in the mid- to late 1930s.

Writing in *Design for To-day* in January 1935, William Tatton Brown identified two trends in the architecture of the period: on the one hand a certain formalism, a stereotyped solution to a problem, resulting from the slowing of the inventive process; on the other, an experimentalism that was more revolutionary. Auguste Perret, designer of the first reinforced-concrete domestic structure, belonged to the former group. Le Corbusier exemplified the latter: rejecting all that had gone before, he plunged into the future to explore the infinite possibilities of the machine age, reversing all the accepted methods of building and pushing mechanical ingenuity to its furthest limits. More to be admired for his architecture than for his propaganda (in Tatton Brown's view) was André Lurçat. He created architecture after a careful analysis of the needs of the people who were going to live in it, adapting it to them, biologically, as the hive to the bee. Lurçat's approach left no room for the architect to sacrifice the inhabitants of his buildings either to his aesthetic fantasies or to private profit. It opened up the way to 'a new architecture – the architecture of the man who has mastered the machine'.

Movements towards Modernism

Where did the new styles come from, and what were the philosophies behind them? New groupings of artists and designers arose all over Europe at the beginning of the twentieth century, with the intention of taking their work forward into the new, industrialized world. The Vienna Secession was founded in 1897 by a group of artists who had seceded from the Vienna Academy of Fine Arts in protest at its conservatism. Secession works used natural images and curving forms but were less extravagantly decorative than contemporary French and Belgian Art Nouveau objects, with their lavishly twisting, winding shapes. Paul T. Frankl (1887–1958), a Viennese who emigrated to the USA, designed furniture with Secession overtones, notably the use of such materials and finishes as red and black lacquer and gold and silver plating or leaf.

One of the founder members of the Secession was the architect and interior designer Josef Hoffmann (1870–1956), who organized one of its first exhibitions. Hoffmann's early textiles and carpets were rigidly geometric and nearly always black and white or monochromatic. He later exhibited ceramics at the Paris Exposition of 1925 and made decorative porcelain wares for the Austrian firm of Augarten. His fellow Austrian, the architect and designer Adolf Loos (1870–1933) was one of the pioneers of Modernism. Of his Haus Scheu, built in Vienna in 1912, which featured flat roofs and stepped terraces, Loos later wrote that 'Someone got up in the city council and demanded that this type of building should be forbidden by law.'

In 1903 Hoffman was co-founder of the Wiener Werkstätte, which made furnishings for some of his notable buildings, including the Palais Stoclet in Brussels. The Wiener Werkstätte ('Viennese workshops') had as its aims the union of artist with craftsman and the elevation of the decorative arts. Its fundamental principle was that of Gesamtkunstwerk ('total artwork') – the creation of cohesive, harmonious, complete interior environments, but within the context of commercial viability. Werkstätte artists, designers and craftsmen worked in a style that was mostly rectilinear at first, but after World War I its severity gave way to a lightheartedness that expressed itself in bright, discordant colours and curving, coarse shapes.

The Werkstätte opened showrooms in the USA in 1922, producing textiles and wallpapers in colourful and amusing designs which were enormously popular. Wiener Werkstätte potters toured the USA with the International Exhibition of Ceramic Art in 1928, and their work had an immediate impact on American artists, reinforced when Viennese designers emigrated to the USA.

Cubism was an art style developed in France in 1907 by Pablo Picasso and Georges Braque. It was characteristically abstract, images being depicted in angular, stepped, sometimes overlapping form, often as though from multiple viewpoints, to give the impression of three-dimensionality. As a movement, Cubism lasted only a short time, but its impact on art and design persisted throughout the twentieth century. An outstanding French architect in the Cubist style was Robert Mallet-Stevens (1886–1945), whose work was characterized by free, contrasting volumes and lively façades with detached areas and reliefs. He built villas (including the Villa Noailles, Hyères, 1923) and a series of private houses at Auteuil (1925–27). Both Mallet-Stevens and his contemporary Pierre Chareau (1883–1950) refused to conform to traditional styles and displayed exceptional originality and awareness of the problems of structure and content in the regrettably few private houses they were commissioned to design. Both also designed furniture, using plastic, metal and chromium-plated tubular steel. Chareau's masterpiece was his famous 'glass house' in Paris. Built of iron and glass on three unevenly superimposed levels, it had a façade of concave round glass plaques and, inside, sliding and revolving doors that could double as cupboards.

The painter Mondrian took Cubism a stage further, freeing forms from any hint of objective reality. He was a member of De Stijl, a Dutch Modernist movement founded in 1917. Its forms were abstract and geometrical, with neutral and primary colours used in place of natural form. Gerrit Rietveld (1888–1964) the Dutch designer and architect, was associated with the De Stijl movement in its early days. Linear and angular forms typified his works, such as his chairs made between about 1917 and the mid-1930s, and the Schröder house in the Netherlands (1924). He preferred wood, but also experimented with tubular steel for his furniture creations in the 1920s.

In Germany, a coalition of designers and industrialists, the Deutsche Werkbund, was formed in 1907 with the aim of furthering art not only as an aesthetic, but also as a moral power – both of which were to lead to economic power. The Werkbund championed the identification and promotion of national types, but was concerned to reconcile this aim with the desire to be modern, hence international. (The Paris Exposition of 1925 represented a similar interplay of potentially contradictory motives.) The Werkbund was disbanded and reformed more than once, experiencing not only political opposition from without, but also tensions from within, principally between those members who promoted practicality and the primacy of form and those who advocated greater artistic and individual freedom.

Walter Gropius (1883–1969), who had become a member of the Deutsche Werkbund in 1910, was the founder of the Bauhaus in 1919, one of the most influential design schools of the twentieth century, dedicated to a unification of the arts and the reconciliation of art with industry. As an architect, Gropius typically designed buildings with lateral windows, which created a horizontal emphasis, and made liberal use of glass.

Established first in Weimar and then transferred to Dessau, the Bauhaus school became the foremost centre of design and production in the 1920s, in which creative use of new technologies and materials was favoured and tradition was rejected. The Weimar Bauhaus had some successes, notably with furniture and textiles, but the output of its workshops was largely individualistic, handmade crafts, unsuitable for mass production. When the school moved to Dessau in 1926, occupying a building designed by Gropius, there was a transition to more commercial production based on standardization and economies of scale. Light fixtures and woven and printed textiles were among the major products of the Dessau Bauhaus, overshadowed only by wallpapers, which were first produced commercially in 1929 and thereafter became one of the main sources of the school's income.

In 1928 Gropius resigned from the Bauhaus to pursue his own architecture and design work. The school was closed down by the Nazis in 1933, and many of its refugee staff moved to the USA. Gropius himself, under pressure from the Nazis, went to England in 1934 and there designed furniture for Isokon before emigrating to the USA to become Professor of Architecture at Harvard University (1937–52). The Bauhaus movement in turn inspired the Modernist strain that pervaded the American decorative arts in the late 1920s and beyond.

Marcel Breuer (1902–81), who was born in Hungary, studied at the Bauhaus and became director of its furniture design department in 1924 before setting up as an architect in Berlin in 1928. He had an extraordinary impact on design with his tubular steel furniture, which he first used

ABOVE: *Buildings erected during the land boom in Miami, Florida, in the 1920s and 1930s.*

OPPOSITE: *The Union Carbide Building on North Michigan Avenue, Chicago, features designs reminiscent of classical styles.*

for the Wassily chair in 1925. His Cantilever chair of 1928, made from a single length of tubing, remains a classic – today it is so familiar as to be thought unexceptional. After a short period in the UK, also working for Isokon, Breuer moved to the USA, where he built his own house and made experimental furniture.

The Isokon company was set up in 1931 to design and build houses and furnishings using new technologies and materials, among them glass. One of its co-founders was the Canadian architect Wells Coates (1895–1958), who settled in England in 1929. He was a key promoter and exponent of the Modernist aesthetic during the 1930s, and the designer of the famous Lawn Road Flats in north London. Although his work was typically Art Deco in its shapes and materials, it bore little or no decoration. On a smaller scale, he designed household objects such as a famous series of Bakelite radios.

The British Design and Industries Association (DIA), founded in 1915, was the forerunner of the Council of Industrial Design (founded 1944) and, later, of the Design Council (1960). It arose out of the Arts and Crafts Movement with the mission to promote design in industry. Its first publication contained the statement: 'The first necessity of sound design is fitness for use.' The DIA moved only slowly towards endorsement of Modernism, but its magazines, *Design in Industry* (1933), *Design for To-day* (1933–5) and *Trend* (1936), made a lively and important contribution to the advancement of that movement.

The movement known as Constructivism emerged in Russia after the Revolution of 1917. Constructivist art was essentially applied art designed for mass production. Pure line, form and colour were its defining features. Works were generally 'sculptural', that is, constructed or assembled rather than carved or painted. Suprematism also originated in Russia and signified the attempt to reduce forms to simple geometric arrangements in pure colours. The term derives from the notion that works so rendered represent 'the supremacy of pure emotion'.

Functionalism was not a movement, but rather a belief that – in the phrase of the American architect Louis Sullivan (1856–1924) – 'form follows function': that is, that an object's purpose should be the prime determinant of its

LEFT: *This block of flats in North London has the characteristic flat roof and square-angled bays of the 1930s.*

OPPOSITE: *A view of the back court of a block of flats in Poplar, east London, early 1930s. The elevated walkways were considered very welcoming, friendly and convenient at the time.*

appearance. Sullivan was the pioneer of modern office blocks and one of the founders of the 'Prairie' school of architecture. Le Corbusier is often cited as functionalism's principal proponent, yet he was also keen to exalt the expressive qualities of an object.

Modernism

The term 'Modernism' designates no particular group of artists or designers, but refers to a general trend away from traditional styles and towards functionalism and economy. The Modernist aesthetic was complemented by ideological strains such as progress, social justice and internationalism. Modernists aimed to produce high-quality, practical and appealing products for the mass of the population. Key features of Modernism in architecture were: the use of modern materials such as reinforced concrete and steel frames with glass infillings; abstraction, functionality and the exposure of structure; and the avoidance of ornament and colour.

Modernists argued that high quality and mass production could be complementary and that the beauty of a building or any other object was defined most precisely by the closeness between its form and its function. The

straight line became a thing of beauty, but only the most ardent of Modernists would deny that tasteful decoration enhanced a design. Moreover, public taste still lingered in the decorative tradition of many previous centuries, so convincingly and popularly evoked by Art Nouveau, and could not so readily make the transition to pure functionalism, whatever the exigencies of the machine age.

Conservatism was particularly strong in the USA, where representational art, often in Classical styles, continued to hold sway. In the 1920s, however, the arrival in the USA of émigré avant-garde artists from Europe and the return of nationals who had trained in Europe contributed to the acceptance of Modernist styles. A third factor that had a major impact was the development of the skyscraper. After 1925, Manhattan-style towers began to appear in many small towns, despite protests about the disharmony of their scale in this context from Frank Lloyd Wright and others. Frank Lloyd Wright (1867–1959) was one of the twentieth century's foremost architects and an important thinker on the subject of design. His own buildings were generally low and simple, blended comfortably into their landscape and were largely made from a variety of natural materials in different colours and textures, usually with open-plan interiors which gave a feeling of spaciousness. His style of 'organic architecture' derived to a great extent from the Japanese, which he had studied and admired. However, he initiated many new techniques, including the use of precast concrete blocks reinforced with steel rods, air conditioning, double glazing, indirect lighting and panel heating.

As time wore on, the Modernist aesthetic became universal, so that by the 1930s it came to be known as the International style. (The name derived from an exhibition, entitled 'The International Style', held at the Museum of Modern Art, New York, in 1932.) This rendered it susceptible to the charge that it was 'selling out to capitalism'. If Modernism failed as a radical programme for world change, in the face of the reality of social disorder, it attempted at least to champion universal human dignity.

The principles of the International style in architecture were the importance of volume, the priority over symmetry of 'organizational concept' and the abandonment of arbitrary decoration. The leading exponents of the International style – Walter Gropius, Mies van der Rohe and Le Corbusier – chose simple, functional forms executed in the new materials: steel, reinforced concrete and plate glass. They eschewed historicism and embraced abstraction, functionalism and technology.

Le Corbusier (1887–1965) was one of the foremost architects of the twentieth century. Born Charles-Edouard Jeanneret in Switzerland, he settled in Paris in 1917 and was creating pioneering works before he reached the age of 30. In 1919, he and the artist Amédée Ozenfant (1886–1966) published a manifesto of Purism, and during the 1920s they headed a group of progressive designers called L'Esprit Nouveau. Their radical pavilion of this name at the 1925 Paris Exposition, a structure of emphatic verticality, was quite different from any previous architecture and had a great impact, both on the public and on other designers (see pages 36–37 for other designs).

Le Corbusier's genius revealed itself particularly in designs for private houses such as the Villa Savoye (1929–31) in Poissy-sur-Seine, France, and in urban architecture. Though many of his designs were rejected by clients, their influence on architects was far-reaching. The concept of cities built on stilts (*villes pilotis*) and the flexible method of unit construction, in which concrete floors are supported by steel pillars, demonstrated in his theoretical 'Maison Domino', were two of his influential architectural ideas. Le Corbusier defined architecture as 'the masterly, correct and magnificent play of masses brought together in light'. Light and purity were the ultimate aspirations of his architecture. 'If the house is white all over,' he wrote, 'the

shapes of things stand out without any possible ambiguity...You might call [white] the X-ray of beauty, a permanent court of judgement, the eye of truth.' Le Corbusier set the trend towards the purist, austere Modernism that rejected the elitism and exclusivity of Art Deco. His objective rationality led him to his famous statement that 'the house is a machine for living in'.

Ludwig Mies van der Rohe (1886–1969) was a German-born architect who emigrated to the USA in 1938, having been the last head of the Bauhaus. Much of his work made extensive use of steel and glass. In the 1930s, he produced innovative cantilevered tubular-steel furniture, of which the best-known item is perhaps the Barcelona chair (1929).

The passion for design

An editorial in *Design for To-day*, written in May 1935, looked back contemplatively over the previous 25 years, concluding that these years had been a transitional period in the history of design, 'preliminary to liberation of the creative spirit in art and industry and in every single phase of design as represented by the achievement of art and industry'. The greatest progress had undoubtedly been achieved in the purely industrial field. In an increasing number of houses the movement was beginning to develop speed, but it had made 'practically no impression on large scale housing schemes…we might be encouraged to believe that housing is providing an example of reversion to type rather than an experiment with new equipment, new designs, new materials and new amenities.'

For these failings the writer blamed the lack of imagination of architects and of the local authorities that employed them. What, he wondered, should be expected in the next few years? A 'very rapid and very widespread adoption of first class design in industrial buildings'. One could 'look forward to more rational planning of living accommodation' and 'a swing of the pendulum away from the elaborate and artificial back to simplicity and clear colour in the equipment and materials necessary for a modern home'. The writer also anticipated the Paris Exposition planned for 1937, a successor to the 1925 Exposition. With admirable but misguided optimism, he wrote that: 'At many points the new world is beginning to emerge and it has a finer and more radiant appearance than the grey, distorted chaos in which the pre-war and post-war generations have lived with ever increasing discontent.' Four years later the world was at war again.

Arguing the case for the abstract artist as an essential contributor of talent to industry, the revered British critic Herbert Read (1893–1968) pleaded for a policy based on aesthetic values, but found no political system in existence that offered such a policy. Soviet Russia, he said, had seemed to promise that ideal state, but had now dismissed Le Corbusier and was reverting to a 'hideous nationalism in architecture and design'. In Germany, another country of promise, the Nazis had suppressed the Bauhaus and driven the best architects and abstract artists out of the country, turning back to traditional and nationalistic forms.

It seemed to Read that reason and sensibility were everywhere being sacrificed to crude nationalistic prejudices, class ideologies and commercial rivalry. He saw hope in one fact only – the inevitable progress of the machine, which, in triumphing, would bring down the structure of the society that made its triumph possible. Then consumption would be adjusted to production, our

'mediaeval money system' would disappear and people would enjoy the age of plenty. Only then would we have the leisure to replan our lives 'with the detachment and disinterestedness essential to any aesthetic activity'. The artist would become, if not the philosopher-king, at least the true captain of industry.

The founder of the Bauhaus, Walter Gropius, thought in equally global but somewhat more down-to-earth terms. His guiding principle was that artistic design is an integral part of life and that the new architecture should progress towards an ever fuller conception of the province of design and construction as one vast indivisible whole. The architect's job would be to resolve all formal, technical, sociological and commercial problems and combine them in a unity that extended beyond the house to the street, from the street to the city and ultimately into the wider field of regional and national planning. He believed that the Bauhaus conception of the new architecture was nowhere in opposition to that of tradition, since respect for tradition was at bottom a struggle for essentials, a struggle to get at what was 'at the back of all technique'.

In Britain it was becoming noticeable that people were developing an appreciation of modern architecture and design, especially among the younger generation. Writing in 1933, Lord Gorell, president of that year's Exhibition of Industrial Art in Relation to the Home, observed in the exhibition catalogue that the three main principles governing successful manufacture were now 'Design, design, design'. In his view, the pre-eminence of design and people's appreciation of it was making a comeback, having been submerged during the time of

> ...the apotheosis of the machine and the turbulence of mass production, in which the master craftsmen perished...One would have thought that anyone turning out any article in vast quantities would have recognised the paramount necessity of ensuring that the initial design from which those vast quantities were made was the best possible – it seems ordinary common sense, and yet it was overlooked. It is now at length regaining recognition.

The architect Serge Chermayeff was much more forthright and angrier, writing in *Design for To-day* of the 'decay of taste. Taste rotting under complacent stupidity, self-deceptive snobbery and spineless sentiment.' He drew some comfort from the fact that ugly, badly designed objects were becoming fewer, and asserted that nothing need any longer be ugly because it was utilitarian, nor bare or cold or uncompromising because it was machine-made. But the habit of disguise persisted. Telephones, for instance, were stuffed under dolls, although the telephones themselves were much more beautiful to look at than their covers. There was some distance to go before modern design would – as it must – express the social and economic conditions of the time.

The advance of modernity

Ernst Freud, a German architect writing in the mid-1930s, found it most surprising, as an outside observer, to discover how very few modern buildings were to be found in Britain. On the whole, he observed, the idea of modern architecture had not yet begun to influence the features of British towns. He concluded that this showed that there were too few modern architects designing modern buildings to be erected. Nor were there sufficient clients inclined to accept and appreciate the principles of modern architecture, such as simplicity of form, planning and conformity with regulations and use, and the structural possibilities of new materials.

There was some resistance in Britain to modern style. 'The simplification of anything,' as G. K. Chesterton put it, 'is always sensational.' The late style of Charles Rennie

OPPOSITE: *The residence of Dr John Storer in Los Angeles. Frank Lloyd Wright designed the house, inspired by Mayan architecture. The Storer House was built of plain and patterned precast concrete blocks 'woven' together with 'threads' of reinforced steel.*

ABOVE: *A prime example of the style of house on display at the* Daily Mail *Ideal Home Exhibition in 1934, which prompted one observer to write that 'This year it's all white, flat-roofed and "different"'.*

Mackintosh, with its geometric decorations, was consistent with Art Deco, but the actual structures had less connection with new architectural styles. The greatest contribution to British housing in the 1920s and 1930s was in simple and largely unoriginal cottage housing schemes. Such houses were not noticeably modern, but were better adapted than any others to the British landscape.

By contrast, in Germany modern building made considerable headway after 1918, when modern architects were appointed 'town architects' and became teachers at the principal high schools. Modern schools, such as the Bauhaus, were subsidized. In Frankfurt and Berlin, new suburbs for the working classes had been planned and built, which Freud termed one of the greatest achievements of postwar Germany. All municipal buildings, such as town halls, schools, hospitals and state insurance companies, were the work of modern architects, and their example in turn influenced state enterprise.

In the case of commercial buildings and factories, the need to be streamlined, efficient and conspicuous (for advertising purposes) chimed in obvious ways with modern construction. As people became familiar with the new forms, welcoming the liberation from historical styles, they began to take an interest in architecture. The tide had turned towards modernity. 'I can imagine,' wrote Ernst Freud,

> ...that some monuments in the next few years may be carried out in the heavy pompous style of the Wilhelmian period, but although Hitler-Germany is so far against the modern tendencies in architecture, accusing them of being international and on account of their connection with the socialist movement, I cannot believe that architecture in Germany will go back to imitating Gothic or Renaissance.

Frank Lloyd Wright's remark that 'architecture begins where function leaves off' was borne out by the experiences of contemporary architects, who realized that it is impossible to impose aesthetic form on new materials: the proper form evolves from their correct use. 'Fitness for purpose' and 'functionalism' embodied two requirements – the solution of a construction problem and the solution of a need problem – which were often mutually exclusive. The architect had to provide answers to needs such as plumbing or insulation, while at the same time putting the non-scientific side of the job into effect. But art was not an add-on; it was the 'doing well of what has to be done'.

There were those who, some felt, took functionality too far. The believers in 'fitness for purpose' and functional beauty (wrote B. J. Fletcher in January 1934) often felt that

> ...they have an unassailable position and dictum. They claim too much. Efforts which are one man thick are not to be set against the beauty which has resulted from aeons of evolution...The design which consists of an assemblage of plate glass and what might be machine parts is an affectation as far removed from 'fitness for purpose' as the vegetable tangle of Victorian designers...[Design] should display the character of the material, not disguise it, nor with one material imitate the characteristics of another...It should be a duet between designer and material, both giving their best, the one the complement of the other...

The architects' desire for freedom to give form and style to the new materials they had at their disposal can be detected

OPPOSITE: *Aluminium lighting fixture designed by Jacques Le Chevalier.*

RIGHT: *Silver tea service designed and made by Atelier Desny, Paris.*

in many of their most famous designs, such as Rietveld's Schroeder House (1924), Gropius's Bauhaus at Dessau (1925–26), Neutra's Lovell Health House in Los Angeles (1927–29), Le Corbusier's Villa Savoye at Poissy-sur-Seine (1929), Mies van der Rohe's German Pavilion at the Barcelona Exhibition (1929) and Alvar Aalto's Paimio Sanatorium (1929–33).

Although architects in different parts of the world travelled along different socio-political trains of thought, they often arrived at the same practical conclusions. The Russian architect Jacob Chernikhov, writing in 1931, believed that

> …ornament is natural to every social class, and in no way can be regarded as proceeding necessarily from a bourgeois-capitalist mentality. Proletarian ornament, or ornament of a proletarian sort, has great logic, it does not involve needless extravagance. Ornament of this kind is natural to proletarian creative work.

In 1930s Britain, the prime basis of controversy was the flat roof (see photographs on pages 28–9). In other respects all modern concrete houses closely resembled each other. The pitched roof of loose tiles was, some said, an anachronism left over from a time when there were no materials that could satisfactorily be laid flat. One advantage of a flat-roofed house was that it could be expanded by erecting a further storey with a minimum of structural or architectural damage. In extending a pitched-roofed house in this way, the major part of the expense and of the structural difficulties would lie in the necessary alterations to the roof (hence the continuing popularity of loft conversions).

Of the *Daily Mail* Ideal Home Exhibition at Olympia in 1934 one observer wrote that 'This year it's all white, flat-roofed and "different"'. The 'difference' lay principally in the fact that builders had co-operated with architects of distinction, who were able to exercise some control over furnishing. Thus the visitors to the exhibition would see, probably for the first time, a house in which space was economically and logically utilized and in which contemporary furniture and fabrics were used to good advantage. Although the reviewer thought the *Daily Mail* was to be applauded for giving due emphasis to design, he regretted that it did not carry its educational policy further and illustrate town and street planning in addition to the design of individual houses.

The exhibitions

The Exposition Internationale des Arts Décoratifs et Industriels Modernes held in Paris in 1925 has been discussed fully in the introduction of this book. A number of other exhibitions of domestic design and architecture were held between the wars. Their dual purpose was to raise the profile of modern design in the eyes of the public and to provide a showcase for industrial advances.

Following the Exhibition of Household Things mounted by the Design and Industries Association at the Whitechapel Gallery, London, in 1920, the British Institute of Industrial Art, which was formed in that year, staged an Exhibition of Industrial Art To-day at the Victoria and Albert Museum, London, in 1923. The BIA had been founded principally to mount exhibitions that would encourage the raising of standards in industrial art and link industry with the activities of museums and art galleries. As such, its first exhibition was a disappointment, the exhibits being largely art-based and conventional.

Industrial production was better displayed at the annual British Industries Fairs (BIFs) organized by the Board of Trade, with the sole intention of attracting firm orders from abroad for British manufacturers and exporters. The BIFs were treated seriously and reported extensively and the orders placed each year gave a good indication of the success of trade.

The British Empire Exhibition of 1924, though huge and much publicized, served the interests of British manufacturers and traders less well. *The Architectural Review* observed regretfully that British industrial art was 'depressingly bad' in design and colour, lacking 'ideas, spontaneity, and tone'.

An international housing exhibition opened in Stuttgart, Germany, in 1927. Its most famous exhibit was probably the Weissenhofsiedlung, which clearly demonstrated the ideas of the Deutsche Werkbund and the associated Neue Sachlichkeit ('new realism') movement.

In 1931, the Berlin State Porcelain Factory held an exhibition of 150 designs to discover the preferences of the public. Of all the designs shown, the two most popular pieces were plain white, indicating, perhaps, a love of simplicity that was ahead of a trend still to come in the USA and Britain.

The Exposition Coloniale in Paris, held in 1931, displayed every aspect of colonial life. Pavilions were erected in traditional native styles. Both fine and applied arts were exhbited, including luxury traditional pieces that appealed to overseas buyers as well as cheaper items for mass consumption.

By 1930, the split between the decorative artists, or *ensembliers*, and the Modernists had become entrenched. The ambitiously titled Brussels Exposition Internationale et Universelle served only to underline this divergence, the Salon des Artistes Décorateurs showing a family setting in one place and the Union des Artistes Modernes exhibiting their radical schemes in another. A further Exposition in Paris in 1937, organized as a sequel to that of 1925 with the aim of encouraging collaboration between art and technology, made no headway in bridging the gap between the decorative and the functional.

Meanwhile in Britain, a decorating firm named Shoolbred's held an exhibition in 1928 of work by the Décoration Intérieure Moderne, a French group that had exhibited at the Paris 1925 Exposition. An Exhibition of Contemporary Art for the Table, held at Harrods store in London, in 1934, showed many ceramic designs by living artists such as Ben Nicholson and Dame Laura Knight. Some of the pieces were visually exciting, but they were beyond the price-range of most people and had little impact on pottery production.

In Britain in the mid-1930s, a number of exhibitions of contemporary design were mounted with the intention of demonstrating to the general public the importance of good design in objects they encountered in everyday life. British Industrial Art in Relation to the Home was held in London in 1933 and British Art in Industry in 1935. Since some of the pieces had been specially made for showing, however, the exhibitions were not entirely representative of industrial production as a whole. Further exhibitions of domestic design were held during the 1930s by the Royal Institute of British Architects and at Whiteley's department store in London.

Slum clearance and housing schemes

Between 1921 and 1931 there was a population influx into the Greater London area of at least 60,000 people per year (some estimates give a total for that decade of one million) and the rate increased between 1931 and 1935. In the rush to supply the need for new housing, it was therefore not surprising that building took place in a haphazard way, in ribbon developments, for example, rather than through the construction of satellite towns or residential zoning.

Things began to improve in the early 1930s. Areas on the outskirts of London, where travel facilities existed and land was relatively cheap, were now the sites for more structured residential areas. Dormitory estates were also built further afield. One such scheme was the Frinton Park estate in Essex, a complete new residential town comprising 1,200 houses in various styles including traditional cottages, Jacobean and Georgian-style houses ranging in price from £600 to £6,000, and houses designed on functional lines utilizing the most modern methods and materials, such as reinforced concrete and glass. The architect, Oliver Hill, was contracted to design not only the general layout of the estate, but also public buildings such as the shopping centre, railway station, town hall and a hotel on the seafront.

New houses like these were cheaper to construct than the original period buildings they imitated, because of the recent general lowering of the cost of domestic electricity. Chimney stacks, flues and fireplaces could all be eliminated, and the money saved in building costs could be invested instead in modern electrical labour-saving devices, such as cookers, refrigerators, panel heaters, immersion heaters and water boilers.

Of course, houses of this kind were intended for the middle classes. Decent homes for the poor were still a rarity. Slums and overcrowding remained in all their horror and misery. Of British attempts to deal with the problem, perhaps the most successful were council house estates in garden cities and suburbs, which were a development of the English village tradition. These were, however, expensive both in land and in material. Cheaper methods of construction were evolving elsewhere in Europe, as were means of supplying local amenities for the 'beehive life' envisaged by André Lurçat.

Elizabeth Denby, holder in 1934 of a Leverhulme Research Fellowship for Slum Clearance, wrote that the British attempt to solve the urban housing problem was rural, sentimental and already obsolete. At best, she thought, official policy might prevent the growth of the slum problem but without making any serious contribution to the root cause – the shortage of supply. The government was contemplating reconditioning and de-crowding 'improvement areas' concurrently with 'slum clearance', a policy likely to perpetuate for many years the 'rows of mean streets which are the miserable legacy of the industrial revolution', while the surplus population would be rehoused in dormitory suburbs 'sprawling unregulated and unplanned over the surrounding countryside at the caprice of the private speculator'. (How little has changed in 70

OPPOSITE: *A copy (1966) of a chaise longue designed in 1928 by Le Corbusier. It is made of chrome-plated and black opaque painted steel, with leather upholstery.*

LEFT: *Chair and table in ultra-minimalist style, designed for Thonet by Ludwig Mies van der Rohe, 1927.*

years.) A 'melancholy example of this indifference to town planning and town growth' was exemplified by London itself, where the absorption of new inhabitants had been conducted haphazardly.

In 1930 the British government passed an act of Parliament designed to rid the country of the worst evils of slums and went on to promise further legislation to deal with overcrowding. Considerable rehousing activity would be a consequence. As much as one-thirtieth of the entire population of England and Wales would have to be physically removed from one house to another under the first part of the scheme alone. Large sums of public money were to be devoted to the rebuilding of towns. A travelling exhibition entitled New Homes for Old (1932–34) was instrumental in rousing public opinion behind the abolition of slums, but – as was rightly observed at the time – slum clearance needed to be considered as only a small part of a general policy for housing. A national policy should include a survey of all related requirements, such as town planning, traffic regulation, location of industry and of schools, preservation of open spaces and the reorganization of the building industry.

MARS (Modern Architectural Research), the group of British architects and allied technicians that came together in the 1930s, had learnt from the experiments in form and function that had been made almost simultaneously in various European countries since the turn of the century and which had led to a new international manner of

building. They had also taken on the notion that the architect assumed certain social responsibilities. MARS set out to perform research that no other organization existed to do. That work included not only technical investigation into planning and structure, but also analysis of the whole structure of society. Its first project was to study slum clearance and housing, and its findings were incorporated into the New Homes for Old exhibition in 1934.

The basis of British rehousing policy was the small house, preferably semi-detached, which was in effect an extension of the rural cottage tradition. In urban slum clearance areas, land values prohibited this kind of rebuilding at a rent working people could pay, and houses were therefore erected in large estates outside the towns. In London and some other large cities, the tradition was modified to permit central blocks of flats to replace central slums. These provided no new way of living, but were merely, wrote Elizabeth Denby, 'cottages above one another, but without the cottage garden or the cottage privacy', and such schemes were 'born obsolete'. Imagination and enterprise, not piecemeal 'improvements', were needed. Whereas costs in the motor car industry had been reduced by 10 per cent between about 1914 and 1934, building costs had risen by 80 per cent. Economies in slum clearance were nearly always achieved at the expense of size, equipment and amenities because of a lack of vision, courage and the will to bring the best of the new within the reach of the poorest people.

In Britain, many houses put up by speculators in the suburbs of the great towns, aided mostly by building societies, were undistinguished, even ugly, although oases existed in the form of garden cities. Even grimmer were the wildernesses of isolated houses such as those that blighted the north-eastern suburbs of Paris. They lacked communications and effective public services, were placed higgledy-piggledy, without any consideration of street alignment, and were pretty well devoid of individual architectural quality.

In the mid-1930s, a new scheme was formulated for housing in Paris, which involved commissioning architects to be responsible for designing whole communities, not just houses. It gave them a fairly free hand in design and layout, while adhering to the principle that building upwards, in the form of tenements of three or more storeys, was justified only if such a policy released large open spaces for recreational and other purposes. Garden cities were out of keeping with French preferences. The architects of the new scheme in Paris made extensive use of steel, reinforced concrete, glass and brick. The results of the scheme were generally good and notable for certain

OPPOSITE: *Dining room of the Pavilion de la Maîtrise at the Paris Exposition, 1925, designed by Maurice Dufrène.*

BELOW: *Bas-relief in the dining room at the Embassy Pavilion, Paris Exposition 1925, celebrating the 'arrival of the Ambassador'. The sculptor was Max Blondat.*

elements not yet to be found in British housing: the incorporation of central heating and individual water heating systems, provision for the evacuation and disposal of household waste, kitchen planning that ensured easy operation and the installation of surfaces designed to do away with unnecessary projections.

Similarly, eleven satellite towns built on the outskirts of Paris immediately after World War I were developed on the most modern lines, with due regard to transport and industry as well as to the needs of the residents. Each town was planned as a unit. The general rules laid down that no building could be taller than the width of the street it faced, nor might the central third of a street be the same height as its two flanks, ensuring a rhythmic variety of elevations.

Dwellings in these satellite towns consisted mainly of blocks of flats, largely undifferentiated except by size and position. Special provisions were made for the old, for single people and for artists. Gas, electricity, central heating, hot water and refuse collection were supplied from a central source, with the result that the whole town remained warm during the winter. A system of refuse disposal was used widely in France: anything that was large enough to enter the aperture under the sink could be disposed of by this means. Hot soapy water would flush the waste down and suction would draw it to the central incinerator for burning. The system, invented in Canada, had still not found its way to Britain by the mid-1930s. Vibrated reinforced concrete was used for the external walls; cellular concrete for the internal walls and partitions; and 'lap', an artificial marble, for the kitchen and staircase wall surfaces and for the sinks.

An interesting contemporary scheme in the Marylebone area of London was a slum-replacement development, roughly square in plan, comprising mostly six-storey blocks of flats. Only 38 per cent of the land was built on: the rest formed a central courtyard planted with trees and shrubs to provide recreational space. Concrete would have been cheaper and more dazzling in its first few months, but the architect, Louis de Soissons, chose brick instead, out of a conviction that brick was the natural and suitable material for London houses – warm in winter, cool in summer, ageing gracefully by virtue of its ability to clean itself, maturing to a good colour and needing no repointing for 50 or 60 years. Wooden sashes were used for the windows, as they required less attention than metal. Durability, economy and quality were the keynotes throughout, particularly the provision of light and air.

The Paris Exposition of 1925 had finally disposed of the romantic and rustic tradition. It had also encouraged architects to seek simple types of construction and to design groups of houses that formed an architectural whole rather than individual cottages.

Chapter 2
The Plan & Façade

Modern architecture is, in its essence, the expression in form – the plastic expression – of a certain philosophy of life…The modern is really only for those who can supply their own life and establish their own values…modern architecture is concerned with the actualities of the present. [It is never] concerned with bluff – unlike the Victorian and the other bad periods, which were never, at any time, realities.

William Lescaze

In the words of Hermann Muthesius, founder of the Deutsche Werkbund, 'to live in a private house is in every way a higher form of life'. The aspiration to live in suburbia stemmed from a rejection of life in the industrialized city. Between the wars, a suburban home became attainable to greater numbers of people than ever before. In its most characteristic form, the private house was a small semi-detached villa with its own front door, a small garden in front and a larger one at the rear. The suburbs gave a sense of proximity to the countryside, but were equally close to shops, amenities and workplaces.

Social change
In Britain, building had all but ceased during World War I and because of this and the ensuing shortages, the country faced a severe housing crisis in 1919. The state stepped in with a campaign of local authority building under the slogan 'Homes Fit for Heroes'. The scheme was terminated in 1921, when economics put a limit on the number of houses the state could afford to build, and private builders took over. From 1923, however, they were aided by a fixed subsidy of £120 per house. Tax concessions brought additional capital into the coffers of building societies, which provided mortgages for home buyers.

The high costs of building materials kept house prices high. Nevertheless, social changes permitted more people

RIGHT: *North London houses, completed in 1935 and pictured that year in an article on modern housing developments in* Design for To-day. *The caption read, 'Note the unfortunate effect of removing existing trees from a site'.*

BELOW: *The same houses today – hardly a forest, but the general outlook is pleasantly softened by trees and well-stocked gardens.*

to buy: notably the increase in numbers, if not in substantial wealth, of the middle classes – which constituted about one-third of the population by 1939, compared with about one-fifth in 1911. In Britain, such white-collar workers were employed in a wide variety of occupations and most were immune to the worst effects of the Depression.

By the 1930s, servants willing to climb six flights of stairs were no longer prepared to work at wages that most people could afford. Now, on the contrary, it was the former servants and other poorer people for whom housing had to be constructed. In fact, the issue had become one of great urgency in most countries of the world – great enough in many cases to remove housing from the hands of individuals and place it instead under some form of state control. Servants did not disappear altogether: most better-off families still employed a cook and a parlour maid. Smaller suburban homes did not have the space for a live-

in maid, nor could the owners easily afford one, but they might still employ a 'daily' or 'treasure' to help with the heavier household tasks.

Private development

The suburbs around London were mainly created by speculative builders, strongly encouraged by the extension of the underground lines. Some builders purchased land even before the tube was extended to reach it. Haymills, for example, began building in Golders Green, in north London, around 1910. They acquired further land when it became known in 1912 that the underground would be extended to Edgware. Work was delayed by the war, but by the time Hendon Central station opened in 1923, Haymills's estate – comprising about 450 large detached houses – had already been built adjacent to it.

After World War I, labour and materials were in short supply. The War Services Homes Commission (WSHC) bought timber mills, tile works and joineries, leased brickworks and also acquired much land, all with the aim of enabling eligible people to buy houses on easy terms. Land was cheap because of the depressed state of agriculture and the absence of restrictions on building. In the 1920s, land cost from £200 per acre (0.4 hectare). Although the figure had trebled by 1939, the price of land was still a small proportion of the total building cost. Building materials soon became standardized and were purchased in bulk, including bricks from Belgium, door and window frames from what was then Czechoslovakia, and cement and sand from local works. Workers received low wages, but were encouraged to work overtime: as a result they could run up a house in three weeks.

The Tudor Walters Report of 1918 recommended minimum standards for workers' housing, including the number and sizes of rooms and floor space. Its specifications set the standards for all houses built in Britain between the wars.

Building societies often worked hand in hand with builders, selling homes at the lower end of the market. In 1924 an average house cost around £800: of that, the WSHC lent £700, which the buyer repaid at the rate of about £3.10.0 (£3.50) per week. By 1935 the cost of building had fallen and house prices ranged from about £400 to £1,500. A house could be secured with a down payment of only £5, compared with some £55 a decade earlier, and repayments had fallen from about £1.5.6 (£1.27) a week to as little as 8s 10d (44p). This was at a time when the national average wage was £2.10.0 (£2.50) a week. Builders, anxious to sell, even guaranteed house buyers' payments.

Between 1919 and 1939, four million houses were built in Britain. The new houses were everywhere, especially on the outskirts of Midland and southern towns to which the new centres of production had moved. Most were semi-detached, with a living room, dining room and kitchen downstairs and three bedrooms above. Electricity and gas supplies were laid on, together with hot and cold running water. All but the cheapest houses had a side alley that gave access to the garden and could, if wide enough, provide space for a garage. Roads and pavements were ready laid on new estates before the residents moved in.

Generally the houses were bought on a mortgage. Whereas fewer than one in ten houses in Britain were owner-occupied before World War I, the figure had risen to more than three in ten by 1939. Builders naturally followed their commercial instincts, trying to fit in as many houses as possible on the available land – about 15 per acre (37 per hectare) – until the 1930s. Then some began to make efforts to preserve existing trees and follow the natural contours of the ground, creating 'garden suburbs'.

BELOW: *Houses on the Joel Park Estate, Wokingham, erected in the 1930s. The advent of electricity enabled chimney breasts and flues to be eliminated from the design.*

LEFT: *Semi-detached houses in London. Note the unusual porthole windows contrasting with the rectangular windows and flat roofs.*

BELOW: *Rounded bays and pitched roofs were typical of suburban housing of the 1930s.*

OPPOSITE ABOVE: *Houses in 'Moderne' style. The front windows curve around the bay in the popular 'suntrap' mode.*

OPPOSITE BELOW: *Stained-glass panels in doors and windows were common in suburban houses built between the wars. Most designs featured stylized floral or geometrical motifs.*

Builders and developers in the interwar years, as now, always presented their plans in the best possible light in their promotional literature. The advertising brochure for Oak Lodge Estate (now Oakwood), north London, gushed:

> In planning the new Estate, Laings [the builders] have taken care to preserve many of the magnificent trees and gardens for the enjoyment of the residents. Restful green verges, shady trees and masses of flowering shrubs will beautify wide roads and footpaths, and it is proposed to reserve for the Council two large areas to be devoted to Public Parks.

Ironically, the same estate was pictured in *Design for To-day* in 1935 with the caption: 'Note the unfortunate effect of removing existing trees from a site.' Sixty-five years later the houses still stand on roads adorned with flowering cherry trees – attractive, but hardly the riot of lush forest promised. And yet Laings was one of the better speculative builders. The firm entered the field in 1930 and gained a reputation for soundness, value for money, simple designs, avoidance of gimmickry, adherence to strict building specifications – and generous plantings (the new gardens were each provided, unusually, with a fruit tree already planted). As alternative inducements to purchase, some developers offered free electrical appliances with newly built homes, such as an iron, fire, vacuum cleaner or kettle.

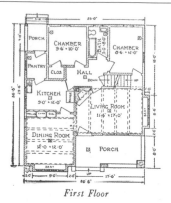

First Floor *Second Floor*

ABOVE AND RIGHT: *Illustrated in the August 1919 issue of* Building Age, *an American magazine for architects and builders, this small house is described as 'A Cozy Bungalow for all the family'.*

RIGHT: *This advertisement for Atlas-White cement appeared in the American edition of* House and Garden *magazine in September 1919 and extols the virtues of cement, claiming that it 'gives you the economical advantages of permanent, fireproof construction, requiring no painting and no repairs'. It goes on to pronounce that cement is so easily manipulated that 'it lends itself most readily to any desired contour, outline or structural form'.*

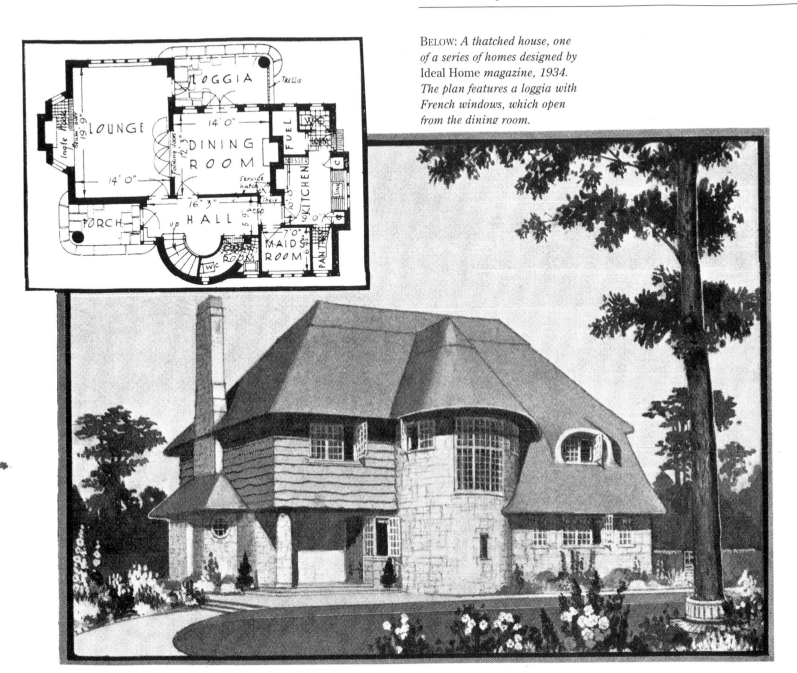

The plan of the small house

In most of the developments in the burgeoning suburbs, architects and planners were dispensed with. Ignoring contemporary trends in architecture and design, most developers chose to build in a familiar, traditional 'cottage' style that appealed to the majority of potential buyers. The houses were consequently the target of much snobbish abuse, then and since, on the subject of their 'bogus' architectural styles. But they remained hugely popular, being unpretentious and welcoming. Most of them had two storeys: the smallest semi-detached houses had a floor area of about 800 square feet (74.32 square metres), although 1,000–2,000 square feet (92.9–185.8 square metres) was more common.

Changes which had occurred in the small house in the early years of the twentieth century included a reduction in the size of the kitchen, thanks to the existence of labour-saving devices, and of the bedroom, with the disappearance of the vast Victorian bed. By contrast, the living room had grown in size, mainly because people simply liked the

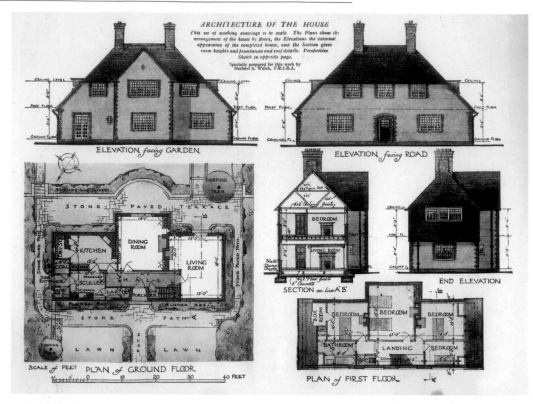

ARCHITECTURE OF THE HOUSE

This set of working drawings is to scale. The Plans show the arrangement of the house by floors, the Elevations the external appearance of the completed house, and the Section gives room heights and foundation and roof details. Perspective Sketch on opposite page.

Specially prepared for this work by Herbert A. Welch, F.R.I.B.A.

ELEVATION facing GARDEN

ELEVATION facing ROAD

SECTION on line A B

END ELEVATION

PLAN of GROUND FLOOR

PLAN of FIRST FLOOR

SCALE of FEET

LEFT: *Plans and elevations of a medium-sized detached house. There are four bedrooms and a scullery, complete with copper, mangle and sink.*

BELOW LEFT: *This bungalow at Esher, Surrey, has an elongated shape but still separates service quarters from bedrooms. It was intended for constant residence, not as a weekend home.*

BELOW : *A medium-sized house designed by Herbert A. Welch.*

OPPOSITE: *'A small house' featured in* The Concise Household Encyclopedia *(1931) as an example of modern architecture. The house was said to be suitable 'for a small family where no resident maid is kept'.*

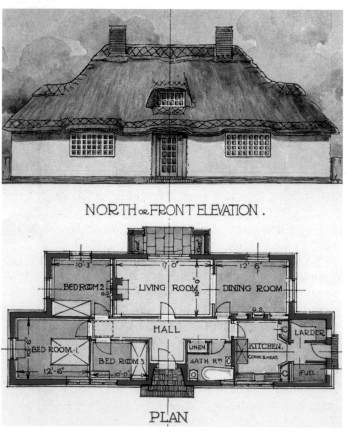

NORTH or FRONT ELEVATION.

BEDROOM 2 | LIVING ROOM | DINING ROOM

HALL | LARDER

BED ROOM 1 | LINEN | KITCHEN COOK & HEAT

BED ROOM 3 | BATH RM | FUEL

PLAN

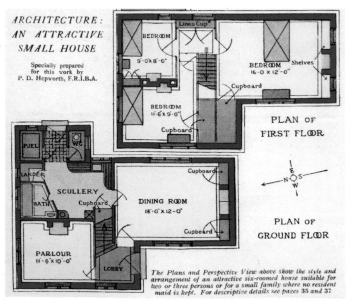

ARCHITECTURE:
AN ATTRACTIVE
SMALL HOUSE

Specially prepared
for this work by
P. D. Hepworth, F.R.I.B.A.

BEDROOM
9'-0"x8'-6"

Linen Cup⁴

BEDROOM
16'-0"x12'-0"   Shelves

Cupboard

BEDROOM
11'-6"x9'-0"

Cupboard

PLAN OF
FIRST FLOOR

FUEL   WC

LARDER

SCULLERY

BATH   Cupboard

Cupboard

DINING ROOM
16'-0"x12'-0"

Cupboard

N

PLAN OF
GROUND FLOOR

PARLOUR
11'-6"x10'-0"   LOBBY

*The Plans and Perspective View above show the style and
arrangement of an attractive six-roomed house suitable for
two or three persons or for a small family where no resident
maid is kept. For descriptive details see pages 35 and 37*

space. There was a paradoxical reason too: built-in furniture, designed for a specific use, actually provided a much greater degree of flexibility in room planning, allowing the architect, for example, to swing back a whole wall to combine two rooms into one, or to create a wall of windows opening onto a terrace. Traditional furniture was in theory movable, but in practice its position in a room was often as fixed as the walls that surrounded it.

Generally, the plan of the semi-detached house was extremely conservative. The entrance hall and staircase were on one side, with the kitchen at the back, and a front parlour and rear dining room on the other side against the shared party wall. Upstairs there were two or three bedrooms and a bathroom with separate WC. In time, the parlour was often removed and the frontages widened to admit more light and air and allow greater access to the garden. Most front walls had a bay, whereas at the back French doors opened out onto the garden. All the rooms were self-contained and private. Each of the reception rooms downstairs was generally more than 10 feet (3.05 metres) square. Of the bedrooms upstairs, two were usually large enough to take two beds while the third would take only one.

The semi-detached or small detached house was typically asymmetrical. A projecting bay ran through both storeys up to a gable on one side. On the other side were the front door and porch under a steeply pitched roof. In the earlier semis, the entrances were in most cases built next to each other to make a pair of houses look like a single house. Later in the 1920s, the entrances were frequently put at the far corners, to create the greatest possible illusion of separation between the two dwellings.

RIGHT: *A cement-rendered bungalow with five rooms. In the mid-1930s it would have sold for about £750.*

RIGHT: *A large country house with shuttered windows, built in the early 1930s. The shutters were painted green to match the roof, which is covered in the green glazed pantiles currently in vogue.*

THIS PAGE: *Two views of a house designed by Leonard W. Last for The* Ideal Home *magazine. The living rooms faced the garden.*

The mock-Tudor style

The interwar houses, or rather their façades and exteriors, displayed an extraordinary variety of decorative and stylistic features. The mock-Tudor 'cottage' style, which drew on some of the characteristics of Arts and Crafts vernacular architecture, was the most popular during the 1920s. Planks were nailed to the gable to imitate half-timbering and the windows sometimes had leaded panes.

The roof was usually brightly tiled and the walls were faced with red bricks, sometimes relieved with pebbledash or hung tiles. The woodwork was often painted in contrasting bright colours, in combinations such as 'Brunswick' green with cream, or dark brown with pale yellow. 'Its decorative aspect,' wrote Mark Pinney in *Little Palaces: The Suburban House in North London 1919–1939*, 'would no doubt seem crowded and restless to an architectural eye, with little of

THIS PAGE AND OPPOSITE: *These houses show various styles popular between the wars. Note the jettied upper storey and imitation half-timbering of the mock-Tudor house (top left) and the very substantial chimney stacks in some of the exteriors.*

the wall plane allowed to show beneath the "features" and yet it tried and succeeded in creating as far as cost would allow an impression of welcoming, cottagey charm.'

In the 1920s, *Ideal Home* magazine launched a publication featuring houses designed by its own team. One of these had a thatched roof – warm in winter and cool in summer – and was faced with elm boarding and stone. The windows were all of different sizes: one sat under a semicircular eave of the roof. Next to the front door was a semicircular bulge in the wall resembling a tower, housing the hall and the staircase. At the back of the house was a loggia (covered patio) with French windows opening on to the garden. A similar area made the entrance porch leading to the front door, which was of oak with iron hinges. Inside, the lounge and dining room could be made into one by throwing open a set of folding doors. The lounge had an inglenook (a fireplace within an alcove), while a service hatch connected the kitchen to the dining room. The whole plan boasted a 'charming irregularity of outline'.

The Ideal Home Book of Plans went into several editions and was a great success, not only among prospective builders but also among homeowners who were keen to increase restricted accommodation, turn a loft into a useful room, modernize the bathroom or make other practical and

OPPOSITE, ABOVE: *A house near Cologne by Hans Schumacher, c. 1933. It was constructed of stone, with steel columns carrying most of the weight. The ground floor is raised, against the possibility of flooding from the River Rhine, which flows near by.*

BELOW AND OPPOSITE BELOW: *White-walled, flat-roofed and 'streamlined', houses like these in the Modernist style appeared in only small numbers in Britain. They were much more popular in Europe where architects incorporated sun terraces on the flat roofs.*

decorative alterations. The keynotes were efficiency, maximizing space and ease of maintenance. One plan was for a small, compact house that was claimed to 'run itself'. Another provided for a loggia and balcony to capture every available bit of sunshine. Both modern and traditional styles (such as Georgian) were included, as were a variety of materials: stone, half-timber, plaster and thatch.

Experiments in Modernism

The mock-Tudor house was enormously sought after in Britain, and the neo-Georgian style also had its adherents – although as it was frequently used for local authority estates it was avoided by most speculative builders, worried that they would not be able to sell houses that looked like council homes. There was also some experimental building in the Modernist style in the early 1930s.

The Warren House Estate in Stanmore, north London, contained one of the largest groups of modern homes in the district. It included a block of flats by Owen Williams and some flat-roofed houses with glass-walled 'sun parlours' on the roofs.

The 'Sunspan' house exhibited at the *Daily Mail* Ideal Home Exhibition at Olympia in 1934 (architects Wells Coates and Pleydell-Bouverie) was designed to have two walls with a southern aspect, so that the sun fell on one side or other of the large living room downstairs, and of the main bedroom upstairs, all day. The living-room fireplace was in

the corner, away from the large windows. The study and dining room were formed by movable partitions and could be joined up with the living room to make one large room. The garage door was under the same canopy as the front door. The kitchen was isolated by a servery from the dining room and the rest of the house. Upstairs were four family bedrooms, a maid's bedroom, a bathroom, shower room and separate WC. The fitted furniture throughout the house was designed by the architects.

OPPOSITE: *Flat-roofed 'suntrap' houses, their horizontal linearity emphasized by decorative parallel lines along the façades.*

LEFT AND BELOW: *Two views of an ultramodern house at Gidea Park, Havering, Essex. These 'cold' sides facing north and east have virtually no windows, while the south and west rooms have large French windows opening on to the roof terrace or garden.*

Among the other 'Houses of Tomorrow' exhibited at Olympia was one designed by Leslie H. Kemp and Tasker of London illustrated on page 61. Its plan was unusual, as were some of the details. The front door opened on to a fair-sized hall, with the living room on the left and the dining room on the right. By opening two sets of folding doors, these three

ABOVE LEFT AND ABOVE: *Suburban houses. The one on the right shows the influence of the International style, but combines it with a pantiled roof and large porticoes.*

TOP: *Concrete houses designed specifically for the seaside. Notice the extensive use of glass, generous windows and French doors, and the protective glass wall for the downstairs verandah.*

ABOVE: *A house in Devon, severe in design, with concrete walls and flat roof.*

spaces could form one 40-foot (12.2-metre) room when required. The living room had a large semicircular window and sun porch, over which extended a balcony from the main bedroom. The house had four bedrooms, one bathroom and a study downstairs. Every part of the house had wireless and electric clocks installed, and there were fitted cupboards and wardrobes throughout.

These futuristic designs were characterized by extending concrete canopies, stepped horizontal lines and flat roofs, although the builders advertised that the designs they exhibited could if preferred be built with tiled, gabled roofs instead of flat ones – perhaps recognizing that, as one visitor to the exhibition wrote at the time, 'Flat roofs and plain coloured-cement walls do not in themselves herald an era of better-designed homes.'

Other innovations

A house built near Cologne, Germany, in 1933 (illustrated on page 52) demonstrated some interesting features. It was made of stone, with steel columns carrying most of the weight. The internal walls had no structural importance, which meant that alterations to the interior, such as moving screens and partitions between rooms, were easy to perform. The walls between the rooms were insulated against sound, while the roofs and terrace were sealed against water and extremes of temperature. As the house was close to the banks of the Rhine, the ground floor had

LEFT: *This detached corner house, built in reinforced concrete 4 inches (10 centimetres) thick, provided large spaces for sun balconies and terraces and had as many open as enclosed rooms.*

BELOW: *An excellent example of a concrete house, with four bedrooms, large living and dining rooms and garage. It would have cost about £1,900 when new in the 1930s.*

been raised to the level normally occupied by the first floor, against the possibility of flooding. At ground level were the garage and other rooms that would not be severely damaged by water.

Pride of place at the Contemporary Industrial Design Exhibition in London in 1934 was taken by a house designed by Oliver Hill as a setting for the display of the best modern domestic equipment, furniture, lighting, floor coverings and decoration (illustrated on page 60). It contained a circular dining room and a living room with built-in fitments and shadowless lighting. The approach to the house was via a pool and sun terrace roofed by a slab of concrete supported by a single circular column. Horizontal lines were the single outstanding feature of the house, emphasized by the curved 'suntrap' windows.

Another prominent architect, Walter Goodesmith, exhibited an all-electric house. The living room, hall, kitchen, laundry and bathroom were all equipped with the latest and most efficient electrical apparatus. Included were glazed lighting panels that could be dimmed to give a soft light, a television receiver, a radiogram and a record cabinet. Goodesmith's design was almost entirely undecorated and relied instead on good balance between the constituent parts and the skilled exploitation of woodgrain.

At the 1933 Ideal Home Exhibition in London, Serge Chermayeff's weekend house was shown in various forms: as a single or semi-detached bungalow, flats or a two-storey

house. The exteriors were starkly simple – rectangular boxes, in essence – with flat roofs and large windows. The 'minimum flat', with furniture designed by Ambrose Heal, was an exact replica of one of the flats in a block designed by the same architect for Isokon Ltd, which was erected in Hampstead in the same year.

A garden house designed in the mid-1930s by Franz Singer as an adjunct to a villa in a Vienna suburb consisted

OPPOSITE: *The uncompromising images of Art Deco were not wholly confined to streamlined 'Moderne' houses. Here, the popular 'sunrays' motif is found in the gate and echoed in the golden-coloured window glass.*

THIS PAGE: *Interwar housing generally fell into two categories of style. At one extreme was the cosy 'olde world' housing mimicking the rural vernacular. In stark contrast was the Moderne type. Curved 'suntrap' bay windows in metal frames, as seen in this bungalow (above), were typical Moderne features.*

of one room of exemplary simplicity, even frugality. Although not meant for living in, the room could sleep two and was wired for heating and lighting. The external walls were of rough oak and the verandah floor was paved with small brown shiny tiles. Inside, the walls were of pine, partly natural and partly polished, and the ceiling was made of dark brown wood. Many of the fitments were dual-purpose or of variable position – a sliding door, a folding door, nesting tables and chairs, a cupboard that could be opened on both sides and a table that could be raised, lowered or extended.

Concrete and its implications

'The real history of the modern movement in architecture,' wrote William Tatton Brown in *Design for To-day* in January 1935,

> is the successive application of scientific method to all aspects of architecture. The first step was taken by Auguste Perret in 1903. He built a block of flats of reinforced concrete. It was the first domestic use of this material… It was so much of an innovation that for two years Perret was the only tenant, living on the top floor in solitude, while the Parisians waited anxiously in the street below for the building to fall down. It still stands.

ABOVE: *Designed by Oliver Hill for the Contemporary Industrial Design Exhibition in 1934, this house is approached via a pool and sun terrace. Inside, it features a circular dining room and living room with built-in fitments and shadowless lighting.*

BELOW: *This traditional design by N. E. Leeson for a pair of cottages was awarded the first prize of £100 in the Building Centre competition in 1933.*

LEFT AND BELOW: *Advertised as a 'House of Tomorrow', this house included a lounge, hall and dining room divided by folding doors that could be opened to make one huge room when required. The advertisement also mentioned that other unusual features included a sunbathing balcony, and that 'wireless is "laid on" in every part of the house, as are electric clocks'.*

GROUND FLOOR	FIRST FLOOR
S=Study	B1, 2, 3, 4 =
L=Lounge	Bedrooms
H=Hall	SB=Sun balcony
D=Dining room	BR=Bathroom
K=Kitchen	LC=Linen
LR=Larder	cupboard
CR=Cloakroom	HT=Hot towel
F=Fuel store	cupboard
SH=Service	W=Wardrobe
hatch	

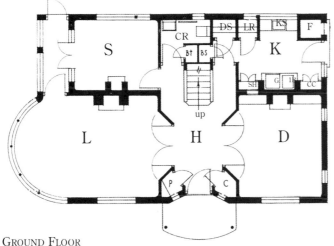

GROUND FLOOR

FIRST FLOOR

LEFT: *This house is designed in what was called 'horizontal style' and, at the time, generally referred to as 'ultra-modern'. It was, however, built using traditional materials: there was no technical reason for the cement rendering over the brickwork, but it was considered an essential ingredient of the 'horizontal style'.*

Reinforced concrete was soon being used as a flooring, walling, roofing and cantilevering material, principally in tank and hydraulic works, bridges, factories and warehouses. When it came to domestic use, there was the question of reconciling the appearance of concrete houses with older buildings in the neighbourhood. Yet by the 1930s a whole generation had been affected consciously or unconsciously by the sight of large simple surfaces, and many were well disposed to architecture that was visibly and unequivocally functional (see photographs on pages 56–57).

Not everybody welcomed the new architecture, however. Professor Harold Hughes, a latterday King Canute, at a conference of the Royal Institute of British Architects in Glasgow in 1935, described the modern movement in architecture as

> ...nothing more than an insidious disease. It is all bunkum...The study of most so-called modern British buildings shows either (1) the influence of America with more or less formal buildings; (2) the latest tricks from France and Germany in reinforced concrete; or (3) the Continental treatment of brickwork...Do the majority of modern buildings give pleasure, or are they sincere? We could still live in perfect comfort in old houses...It is the same everywhere...Streamlining in 99 cases out of 100 is an affectation and adds nothing to speed.

Though still comparatively little used in domestic building, reinforced concrete was becoming the prime liberator in terms of the provision of living space, because of its capacity to span wide openings and its general flexibility. Designers could now regard space as something they could control – impossible in brick, stone and timber construction, where spans were limited and the units of building small. Modern architecture, exemplified in the buildings of Mies van der Rohe and Le Corbusier, was strongly horizontal, a logical outcome of reinforced concrete construction with its slight piers, solid floors, thin membrane walls and large areas of glass. The pitched roof was replaced by a flat deck, tying in with the terraces at ground level and performing specific functions in the 'machinery' of the house. Post and slab construction was capable of changing the whole course of architecture. Costs were about the same as in conventional construction but fell with standardization. In Germany and the USA, the house of standard units had already been worked out in detail by the mid-1930s. In Iceland, 16-centimetre ($6^1/_2$-inch) reinforced concrete walls lined with cork successfully protected houses against the stormy winter weather.

THIS PAGE AND OPPOSITE: *An apartment block built in the Moderne style – the speculative builders' answer to Modernist architecture. Large, narrow 'suntrap' windows set into façades of smooth white rendering were one of the hallmarks of the style and were evocative of the great ocean-going liners built in this era.*

One of the first, if not the earliest, reinforced concrete house in Britain was 'High and Over' by Amyas Connell, built in 1931 in Amersham, Buckinghamshire. A smaller variant by the same architect followed at Haslemere, Surrey. The design and character of these houses arose logically from the use of reinforced concrete: neither could have been constructed in brick without altering the design. Both were built on the cantilever principle, which meant that the various walls did not support the weight of the building, but instead the upper floors and roofs were reinforced with steel rods and were 'hung' or cantilevered

THIS PAGE AND OPPOSITE:
Examples of blocks of flats from Liverpool (opposite above and below right), Manchester. (above), Hembrugstraat, Amsterdam (opposite, below left) and east London (right). In an article on town planning in Design for To-day, *1935, it was advocated that 'the usual roof gables and arrangements are suppressed and flat roof terraces are provided away from street noises and dust, for recreational purposes, sunbathing etc.'*

THIS PAGE: *Suburban blocks of flats in Britain were built in a range of styles similar to the housing of the period. The Moderne block (right) features sun terraces on two levels.*

THIS PAGE: *A variety of designs of railings and parapets, in iron or brick. The railings display typical Art Deco motifs – zigzags, chevrons and curves.*

from one or two reinforced walls or columns. In the Haslemere house the upper floors were cantilevered from walls on the north and east of the house and from six concrete columns. The weight of the staircase was borne by two reinforced concrete columns. This method of construction made possible glass walling to the staircase and windows to the main rooms that cut right across the width of the walls, which were not weight-carrying but merely served as 'curtains' or weather screens.

A similar house in Kent had the upper floor and flat roof cantilevered from the wall on the north elevation and from the walls of the outside staircase. The architect could thus provide wide, light windows that came right up to the ceiling, and wide French doors leading from the dining

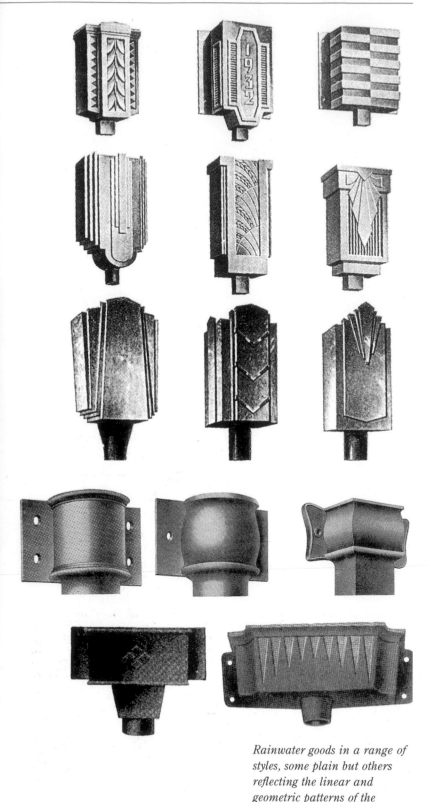

Rainwater goods in a range of styles, some plain but others reflecting the linear and geometric patterns of the building exteriors.

annexe to the garden. Upstairs, next to the outside staircase and balcony, was a bedroom or sleeping porch. Here, instead of solid walls, were wide doors that folded to one side so that the whole wall could be thrown open. The Kent house pointed the way back to the past and forward to the future. It incorporated some features associated with old houses of Tudor times or even earlier – for example, the outside staircase and the overhung upper floor. But it also indicated some future trends, including the use of coloured concrete – in this case a medium green that harmonized well with the rural setting.

In the earliest concrete houses, condensation on the interior walls caused trouble. Two ways of overcoming this difficulty were developed. One was to use two different mixes for the interior and exterior. The two mixes could be poured together if a wire mesh was included in the shuttering. The mesh prevented serious displacement of the two mixes while enabling them to flow together sufficiently to ensure homogeneity. The other, simpler method was to line the interior walls and ceilings with a 1-centimetre (½-inch) layer of insulating wallboard, which was placed in position before the concrete was poured and was thus fixed immovably to the outer concrete. The wallboards had the added advantage of counteracting extremes of temperature.

As to costs, it was difficult to estimate the differential between these concrete houses and their equivalents in brick, although it was clear even then that concrete was especially suited to mass production, from which economies of scale would derive. Moreover, concrete was strong, durable and cheap to maintain, suggesting that its use would become commoner as architects and builders warmed to its possibilities and house buyers became familiar with its advantages.

The Moderne style in the suburbs

White-walled, flat-roofed and 'streamlined', houses built to Modernist designs appeared in small numbers around Britain. Though mainly built in brick, they echoed the style of architecture that had evolved elsewhere in Europe specifically for expression in reinforced concrete. Such houses were designed in the so-called 'horizontal' style and were regarded as being 'ultra-modern'. They usually had long windows without mullions or upright divisions. The exterior was generally rectangular and shorn of mouldings or ornament. They found little favour, being thought 'foreign' and 'bizarre'. Almost all date from a short period in the early 1930s.

Some elements of the International style did, however, find their way into many houses of more traditional design.

They were usually decorative additions to the standard semi-detached house, such as white stuccoed walls and bay windows with horizontal glazing bars. Internally, however, the layout of the houses built in the 'Moderne' style remained unchanged: the open-plan designs of contemporary architects had little impact on suburban house-building.

Details such as brilliantly glazed blue or green pantiles or Spanish wrought iron were acceptable concessions to European styles. In the 1930s there was a vogue for glazed, coloured pantiles, probably initiated about 30 years earlier when green pantiles were brought from Spain for the roof of London's Savoy Hotel, but also stemming from the Californian version of Mexican style imported from Hollywood via the cinema. By the 1930s such tiles were being manufactured in Britain in many colours and looked good on a stone or distempered house. The early developers of Moderne-style houses, finding them hard to sell, quickly modified their designs to make them more appealing to the public – a common compromise was the addition of a pitched, tiled roof.

The sheer white concrete walls of the Modernists were interpreted in the suburban house using white-painted rendering over brick. The emphasis on horizontal lines, reminiscent of the great ocean liners of the day, was achieved with the horizontal glazing bars of metal window frames, which often extended around the bay in 'suntrap' style, sometimes glazed with curved panes of glass, designed to receive as much sunlight as possible in the front rooms of the house.

The Sunspan house displayed at the Ideal Home Exhibition of 1934 vividly expressed the British craving for sunlight. From the 1920s, exposure to the sun began to be seen as beneficial and suntans became fashionable. A contemporary writer suggested that in future houses might be set on turntables so that, like a sunflower, the building

THIS PAGE: *Examples of ironwork balcony railings designed in 1925.*

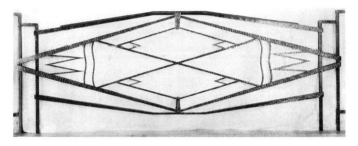

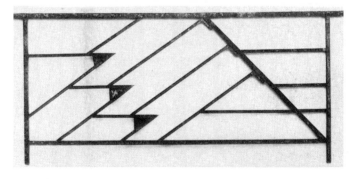

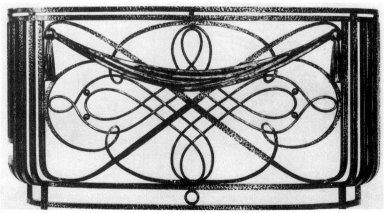

THIS PAGE AND OPPOSITE: *Gables and parapets in Moderne and traditional styles. The one at the top of this page features the popular 'sunburst' design.*

could follow the sun through the day. Another (in *Design for To-day*, November 1933) hoped that in future less would be said about the negative aspiration of 'smoke abatement' and more about 'sunlight getting', in the context of 'the habit of sun-bathing and the popularity of sunburn'. He continued, more sensibly:

> The first barrier to the sun is the smoke-laden atmosphere, which it cannot penetrate at all. That will disappear when we are civilised enough to use smokeless fuels. The other is our walls and windows. We must design our houses with windows large and high enough to admit the sun, using glass that admits the beneficial rays.

The reality was less attractive than the fantasy. White stucco cracked after battling through a few English winters and metal window frames corroded. Most important, the sun disobligingly failed to shine and owners of sun roofs found it more practical to roof them over to create an extra storey. Indeed, by the 1930s it was already recognized that up to a third of the cubic capacity of the average house was 'wasted'. The solution, then as now, was to convert the loft, to which access was gained by a loft ladder.

The British obsession with the sun did, however, leave its mark in the ubiquitous sunburst motif that decorated front gates, gable ends and garage doors. Other decorative details that found their way on to the façades of Moderne houses were restricted to geometric motifs, such as

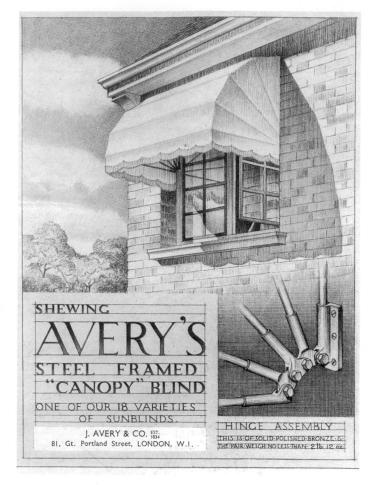

SHEWING
AVERY'S
STEEL FRAMED "CANOPY" BLIND
ONE OF OUR 18 VARIETIES OF SUNBLINDS.
J. AVERY & CO. EST. 1834
81, Gt. Portland Street, LONDON, W.I.

HINGE ASSEMBLY
THIS·IS·OF·SOLID·POLISHED·BRONZE·&·
THE·PAIR·WEIGH·NO·LESS·THAN· 2 lb. 12 oz.

SUNBLINDS OF EVERY DESCRIPTION

chevron or diamond glazing bars, or horizontal bands of contrasting colour on the walls, which accorded with the streamlined Art Deco style.

Flats and apartments

By 1919 many city-dwellers in Europe and the USA had moved into comparatively small apartments, reducing the business of living to a minimum of exertion, but the British continued to resist living in flats. In the 1930s, however, the working classes had to be provided with affordable accommodation near their workplaces and, as land in inner cities was expensive, the building of blocks of flats became a necessity. Many socialist councils put up large blocks in areas of London and other towns and cities. They drew their inspiration from Europe, especially Vienna, where similar huge developments such as Karl-Marx-Hof had been built for workers in the 1920s. These residences were not cheap to rent, costing more than the mortgage for a

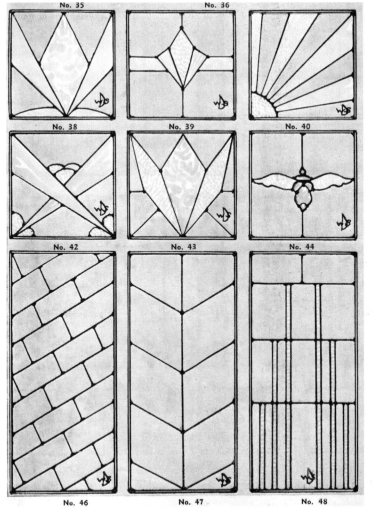

THIS PAGE: *Windows in several styles, including designs for leaded lights (left) from a manufacturer's catalogue of 1928. Casement windows were particularly common between the wars.*

OPPOSITE: *Sunblinds were popular, in spite of the general absence of fierce sunlight in Britain.*

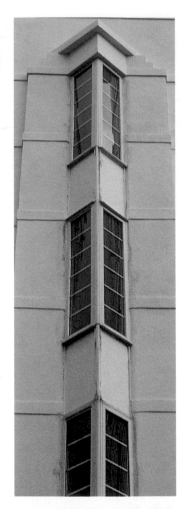

THIS PAGE AND OPPOSITE: *Windows featured small panes in many different styles, from leaded lights and stained glass in mock-Tudor houses, to the* *curved glass and strong horizontal emphasis of the Moderne style, often accentuated by decorations on the surrounding walls*

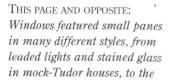

house, but they were convenient for their location and their ease of maintenance. Builders liked to make much of their labour-saving qualities, which included built-in kitchens, central heating and electric fires. The exteriors of the blocks often mimicked Georgian or Modernist styles.

Space constraints naturally created new room layouts and living practices. Small families questioned the practice of wasting a perfectly good room on eating and opted instead for a small breakfast room or for a living and dining room combined.

Interwar house style in Australia

Australian architecture was subject to the influences of English and American styles – including that of Hollywood – as well as its native idiom, which included the use of indigenous materials and reflected what has been called the 'psychology of isolation'. In the 1920s, two styles of house predominated: the California single-storey house (not called a bungalow in Australia) and the Spanish Mission style.

The California house was typically a low, single-storey structure with a high-pitched roof, built of timber or brick, the latter often faced with stucco or pebbledash, wide eaves, roughcast walls, pylon-like chimneys and pillars and many small windows. Two squat columns supported the flat roof of the front porch. A distinctive feature was the placement of the chimney to the main room against the front wall.

The Spanish Mission house also had its provenance in California. It had a roof of Cordova tiles, thick walls covered with cream stucco trowelled to imitate adobe, twisted columns, arched openings, projecting beams and wrought iron. One of the first and still the finest of such houses was 'Greenway', the home of Professor Leslie Wilkinson in Vaucluse, Sydney. He emigrated to Australia from Britain in 1922 and became Australia's first professor of architecture.

Competition arrived in the 1930s in the form of Art Deco styles with decorative patterns of zigzags and wavy lines, effects stolen from Cubist art and the silhouettes of skyscrapers. The mock-Tudor style was also popular, especially in Melbourne. Some more pretentious houses reverted to the Georgian style, which was where Australian architecture had started.

By the end of the 1930s, the beginnings of an Australian style were appearing, partly as a result of the influence of notable architects such as Robert Joseph Haddon and Harold Desbrowe Annear. Haddon moved to Melbourne in 1900. Although he often used Art Nouveau touches in his work, he believed in the precept 'Never be afraid of simplicity'. 'Nothing,' he wrote, 'can be more fatal to successful ornamentation than its excess.' Annear welcomed experiment, advocating 'simple buildings of true

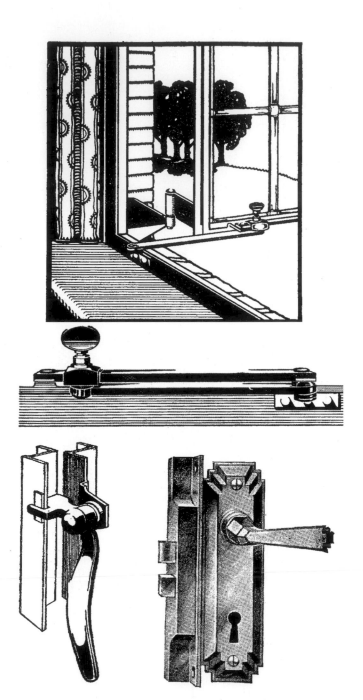

purpose'. Scorning tradition, he observed that 'Real architects have always been and must be inventors in mechanics, in form, tone and colour'.

Walter Burley Griffin, the architect of the Australian national capital, Canberra, designed a model suburb in 1927. The houses were to consist of low, square masses, built of stone or concrete blocks, with windows of various

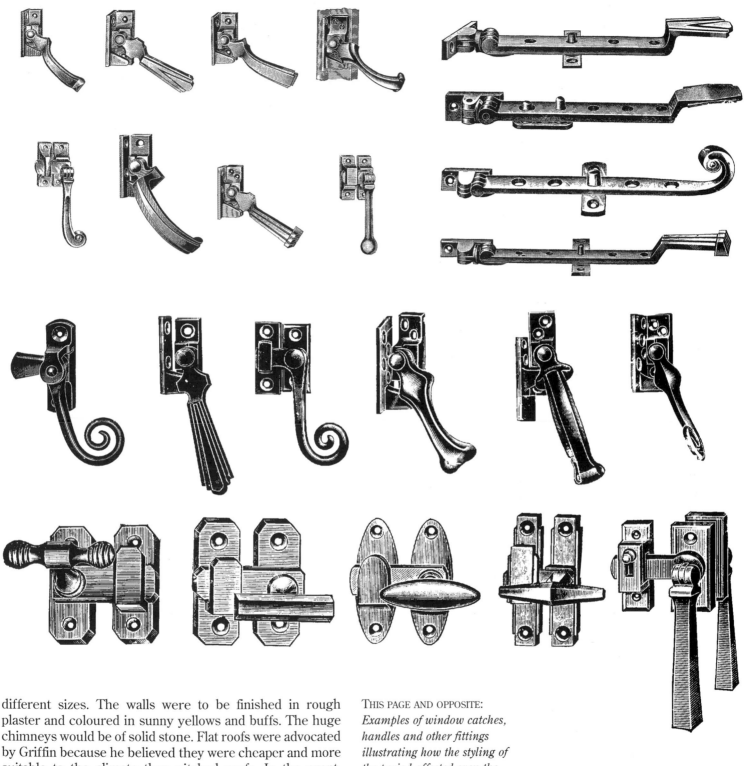

different sizes. The walls were to be finished in rough plaster and coloured in sunny yellows and buffs. The huge chimneys would be of solid stone. Flat roofs were advocated by Griffin because he believed they were cheaper and more suitable to the climate than pitched roofs. In the event, however, plans for the suburb, in Castlecrag, Sydney, were frustrated by the Depression.

THIS PAGE AND OPPOSITE:
Examples of window catches, handles and other fittings illustrating how the styling of the period affected even the smallest detail.

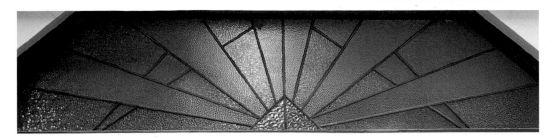

THIS PAGE AND OPPOSITE: *Pictorial scenes, geometric shapes and sunbursts abounded in interwar window designs.*

In Queensland, the typical house was built of timber and raised on long stilts to facilitate air circulation, deter termites and protect against floods. It was also thought that women would be safer inside such houses.

The cost of workers' housing was kept low by the use of fibrous plaster. The technique of making plaster sheets reinforced with flax was invented in New Zealand and introduced into Australia in 1916. It was much easier and quicker to fix fibrous plaster sheets to walls than to use the old lath-and-plaster method. By the 1920s, fibrous plaster was being used all over Australia for interiors. Its extensive use is still peculiar to Australia and New Zealand.

Red Marseilles terracotta tiles became a characteristic of the roofs of Australian suburbs from the 1890s onwards, displacing the once-universal grey slates. Even corrugated-iron roofs were painted red to imitate the tiles. When imported shipments were suspended during World War I, the firm of Wunderlich began making tiles in Sydney. By 1916, the company was turning out three million tiles a year. When concrete tiles appeared in 1920, they were treated to resemble them. Not everyone liked them: the architect Hardy Wilson described them as 'a calamity for Australia'.

The 'servant problem' reared its head in Australia too, encouraging more people to move to easy-maintenance flats. During the Depression, red-brick blocks of flats multiplied fast, especially in Sydney, spreading out from King's Cross to the eastern suburbs and the north shore. The blocks were usually three or four storeys high and contained ten to twelve three- or four-roomed flats. In 1921 Astor Flats, a thirteen-storey block designed by A. S. Macdonald and still standing in Macquarie Street, was claimed to be the tallest reinforced-concrete frame building in Sydney. Because of a height restriction introduced in 1912, no significantly taller building was erected until after 1957. Meanwhile, structural steel had established itself as the normal material for buildings over six storeys high.

Portable houses

Prefabricated houses could be purchased by mail order – not only dog kennels, garages and play-houses, but also complete bungalows and cottages – and assembled by the buyer. In the early 1920s, a prefabricated bungalow or shack was probably the cheapest form of home ownership. Such structures became less popular as permanent houses became cheaper towards the end of the decade. In 1934 in Britain a portable chalet could be bought from £10 4s 6d (£10.23) and a bungalow from £170. One manufacturer was Browne and Lilly Ltd of Reading, Berkshire. Rubber-type roofing was recommended, especially for sheds and outhouses, to protect and waterproof roofs. It could be had in the form of tiles finished in crushed natural slate.

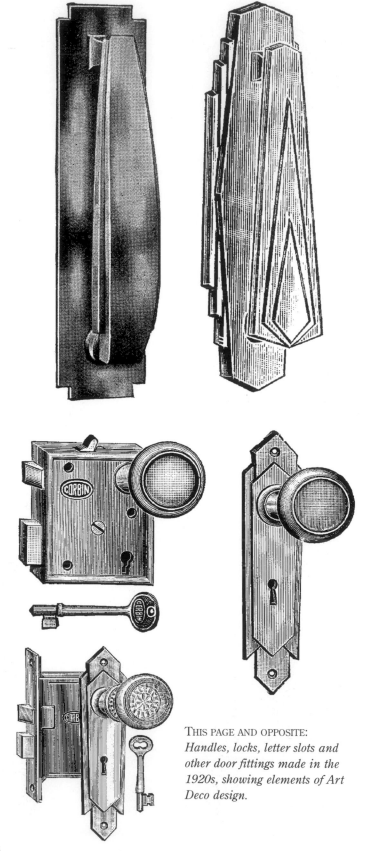

THIS PAGE AND OPPOSITE: *Handles, locks, letter slots and other door fittings made in the 1920s, showing elements of Art Deco design.*

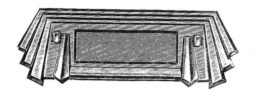

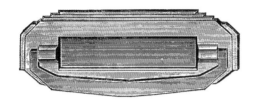

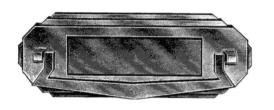

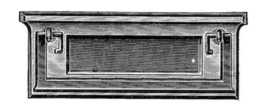

THIS PAGE AND OPPOSITE: *The designs of some doors and doorways hark back to earlier eras, while others are strictly Moderne. Even garage doors did not escape decoration with the 'sunburst' motif.*

Garages

Garages might have partly glazed double doors that opened outwards. Where city ordinances forbade the use of outside swung doors, they were sometimes supported by rollers and when they opened they folded inwards in a concertina shape. Hardware available included holders to prevent garage doors from slamming.

Gardens

The front garden of the suburban British house was usually separated from its neighbour by a privet hedge, sometimes topped with iron chains. Back gardens had fences or walls and, although these were higher than the hedges in front, homeowners still often wanted more privacy and built them up to as much as 8 feet (2.5 metres). The half of the back garden nearest the house was usually occupied by a lawn edged with flower beds, perhaps with a crazy-paving path. Popular varieties of flowers included standard roses, lobelias, alyssum, begonias and geraniums. Pergolas were popular, as were garden ornaments such as gnomes, animal statuettes, sundials and birdbaths. Vegetables were grown at the far end of the garden.

Baird Dennison, reviewing the 1934 Ideal Home Exhibition in *Design for To-day*, referred in the most disparaging terms to the garden furniture on display:

Another presence from which no section [of the exhibition] offers escape is that of quaint rustic seats

and garden benches. Perhaps these innumerable sham wine-casks and wobbly lengths of artily-stained tree-trunks were flotsam and jetsam salvaged from a modern luxury liner that foundered through excessive olde-worldiness.

Swimming pools were made of reinforced concrete, the surface rendered with fine sand and cement. Excavated soil and rock could be used to form a bank on which a wind-screen of trees could be planted. Steel steps could be installed or steps could be excavated or cut from a tree stump. Imperial Chemical Industries issued a booklet setting out means of treating water from springs, streams and wells for use in private swimming pools.

Garden fences and gates could be made of wrought iron, sometimes in elaborate designs, or of simple woven wire to define the boundaries of garden plots. Another combination of fencing materials was English chestnut pales and fine galvanized wire. Interwoven 'chequerboard' fencing promised durability and quality. Willow screening, hazel wattle or willow hurdles and interwoven fencing were available. Entrance gates could be obtained in planed oak, pitch pine, red deal or deal creosoted under pressure.

BELOW: *Ironwork using stylized floral and geometric forms, from the Paris Exposition of 1925, by Baguès Frères (left) and G. Vinant (centre) at the Pavilion of Elegance, and by Decrion (right) at the 'La Stèle' Pavilion.*

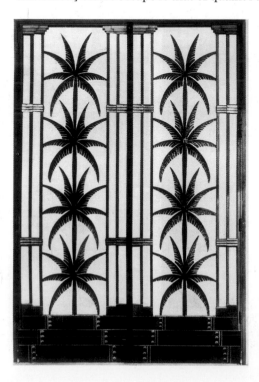
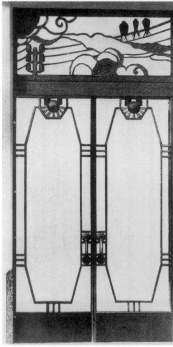

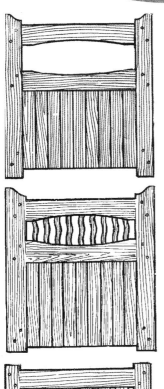

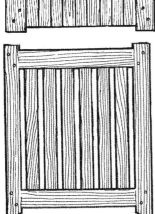

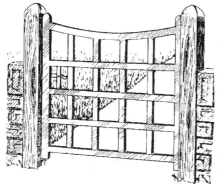

THIS PAGE: *Garage doors and garden fencing and gates.*

Chapter 3
Interiors

Houses are built to live in, and not to look at: therefore let Use be preferred before Uniformity, except where both may be had...You shall have sometimes fair Houses so full of glass, that one cannot tell where to become to be out of the sun.

Francis Bacon, Of Building, *1612*

OPPOSITE: *The shiny black, rectilinear fireplace dominates this otherwise delicately decorated room.*

BELOW: *This colourfully decorated room displays a distinctly oriental flavour.*

In the interwar years, the middle classes increased in numbers but enjoyed only modest means. Consequently, many people preferred to 'do up' their homes in economical ways rather than to move. Interiors tended to be dark, as coal fires were still common and created vast quantities of dirt. In the speculatively built houses of the suburbs, buyers were given little choice in the initial decorative scheme. Exteriors were nearly always painted in two colours and all interior woodwork was either brush-grained or painted a stone colour to provide a suitable undercoat for subsequent graining. Ceilings were distempered in white and bathrooms and kitchens were given a coat of matt oil paint chosen from a limited colour range – typically cream, eau-de-nil green or duck-egg blue. For other rooms, builders were prepared to offer a choice of wallpapers.

As has already been indicated, the pure Art Deco mode of interior decoration was a rarity, in Britain at least. In *Little Palaces: The Suburban House in North London 1919-1939*, Mark Turner has written:

> In all the years I have spent looking at untouched interwar houses, I have never once seen an interior that was the riot of Art Deco Moderne which museums and television would have us believe was typical. Very few suburban residents could buy all their furniture new and immediately. Pieces were

acquired as money allowed, and Modernism was felt to be more appropriate for easily replaceable wallpapers and mats.

In many ways, the ordinary interwar semi represented the final manifestation of mid-Victorian taste in decoration and household management. Such practices included the use of

LEFT AND OPPOSITE: *Examples of Art Deco entrance halls, staircases and banisters. Both wood and wrought iron were popular. Note also the variety of floor coverings.*

colour and graining on woodwork and of linoleum on floors. People still tended to reserve their living rooms for use on Sundays and special occasions.

Social changes that had occurred since the early years of the century had had an enormous impact on the home environment. Along with the increase in the middle classes went a reduction in family size and the virtual disappearance of domestic servants. Few houses built between the wars were designed with servants in mind. In addition to the home management that had traditionally been her province, the housewife, aided by technology, now did the menial work too. Though doubly burdened in this way, she was also expected to maintain her femininity and cheerfulness. Indeed, housework was portrayed by the manufacturers of the new 'labour-saving' equipment as something to be enjoyed.

The 'servant problem' was rendered obsolete mainly by the advent of electricity for home use. Gas was already established as a reliable source of power but in the interwar period electricity gradually became cheaper than both coal and gas, as well as offering other benefits. Electricity was favoured especially for lighting and for powering small appliances such as toasters, kettles and irons. This

development made it necessary to redesign the house, especially the kitchen, which became smaller but more efficiently arranged, even to the point of shrinking into a 'kitchenette'. The availability of hire purchase enabled the less well-off to buy the new domestic appliances. The advent of cheap, tinned food made a pantry less essential than it had been before, although many interwar houses were still built with one.

In order to promote hygiene, which was a major preoccupation of the time, builders incorporated easy-to-clean surfaces in the new houses. Gas or wall-panel electric fires began to replace coal fires. A plumbed-in bathroom suite and a separate lavatory were further requirements.

The race into the future was not headlong everywhere. In Britain in the 1920s and early 1930s, most people could not afford to buy the latest furniture and their homes were often a mixture of heirlooms, hand-me-downs and bargains. When they did buy new furniture, they tended to go for reproductions of historical styles, which gave them a pleasing feeling of connection with great and romantic periods of history. Manufacturers offered furniture in traditional designs but were also beginning to use some of the newly available light-coloured 'Empire' woods, made up

to designs with 'modern novelty features'. Some of the most exclusive modern furniture was made from reed.

Betty Joel was perhaps the most exclusive new designer in the 1930s, selling signed rugs and luxury furniture with large rounded curves. Arundell Clarke, reputed to have created the large square armchair, produced furniture on simpler, more functional lines. Curtis Moffat, who opened his shop in 1929, and Duncan Miller, along with Joel and Clarke, catered for the top end of the market. PEL Ltd made steel-frame chairs and steel and glass furniture. The

THIS PAGE AND OPPOSITE: *Entrance halls often featured lavish designs. A small table, usually set against a wall, was a common feature.*

R & D Davidson Limited

Makers of Simple Furniture produced items in plywood. Jack Pritchard of Isokon Ltd, a friend of Walter Gropius, made perhaps the best steel-frame furniture in Britain.

Plan Ltd produced inexpensive basic units for built-in furniture, much in demand with the shift towards smaller houses and flats. Furniture was tailored to a room so as to occupy the available space in the most economical yet still attractive way. A Swedish idea was a bedroom corner, in which the bed and wardrobe formed a single rectangular unit. The bed, which could be screened off by curtains, abutted the back of the wardrobe, on the side of which was a full-length mirror.

In the early 1930s, however, the British had not yet significantly taken to built-in furniture, despite its obvious advantages in making better use of the available space than was possible with unfitted furniture not specifically intended for the room. One small disadvantage of a complete-concept room with built-in furniture was that it bore the stamp of the designer's or the owner's taste and was difficult for subsequent occupants of the house to change.

In Germany the main sources of innovative design in furniture came from the Deutsche Werkbund and the Bauhaus. The Thonet factory, which had been turning out elegant bentwood chairs for many years, continued to bring out new designs in the 1920s and 1930s, including Mies van der Rohe's chairs of cantilevered tubular steel. Marcel Breuer, who became head of the Bauhaus in 1928 after its move to Dessau, created a number of notable tubular-steel models, including seating and storage. His famous Wassily chair was manufactured by Standard-Möbel from 1926.

A moulded plywood chair with a light metal frame, based on a prototype by Marcel Breuer and built by Saarinen and Charles Eames, won first prize in an international furniture design competition in 1939. In Sweden itself, innumerable designers, working generally to the tenets of functionalism, were producing sensible, well-made and reasonably priced furniture for the mass public. In Denmark, Magasin du Nord in Copenhagen was the source of some interesting new designs. Bentwood and plywood predominated in the functional furniture of the Finnish designer Alvar Aalto (1898–1976).

R & D Davidson Limited

RIGHT: *Spiral staircase designed by Le Corbusier for an apartment in Paris. The perpendicular pivot is of glass.*

BELOW: *A charming landing with a circular balustrade conforming to the curve of the outer walls. The house belonged to a London interior designer.*

When Australian houses began to be all-electric, they had light in every room, plus power points for radiators, fans and an electric iron in the kitchen. Simple, unornamented furniture – in the so-called Mission style – completed the hall. 'Modern' furniture was introduced by Frederick Ward in 1927. He particularly liked raspberry jam wood, a dark red Western Australian variety of wattle that smelt like raspberry jam, and Australian walnut (one of the laurel family). Chrome-plated tubular steel was made in Australia from 1933 onwards and quickly became a symbol of fashionable modernity. White enamelled furniture was popular in bedrooms.

LEFT: *This is the staircase leading down from the landing shown on the opposite page. The handrail is wrought iron painted ivory.*

BELOW LEFT: *As smaller houses put floor and wall space at a premium, 'bespoke furnishing' became a valuable idea. This wall cupboard, built to fit the available space, is ideal for both storage and display.*

Swedish modern furniture became popular in the USA in the 1930s. One example was a chair formed of one sweeping curve resembling a deck-chair, with a seat of canvas strips. Functional forms in blond woods were characteristic. Florence Knoll, Mies van der Rohe and Eero Saarinen designed furniture for Knoll International in styles derived from Sweden and from the Bauhaus.

Entrance halls and staircases

In the British suburban house of the 1920s and 1930s, it was still considered essential that each room should have separate access from a central hall. The entrance was also important in conveying a first impression of the house, and it was desirable for the area to be large enough to allow a turn at the foot of the stairs, which extended the decorative potential of the newel posts and balustrades. In houses in Moderne style, synthetic materials, which simulated marble but had sawdust and asbestos for their main components, could be used for stairs. For the balustrade, a wrought-iron frame might be coated in cellulosed ivory and verdigris. Long staircase windows might include stained glass panels using Art Deco chevrons or geometric motifs.

The fluid curve of the spiral staircase was a feature of some distinguished Art Deco buildings of the period, such as Erich Mendlesohn's De la Warr Pavilion in Bexhill-on-Sea, East Sussex (1935).

Dining rooms

The dining room shrank in the new houses of the interwar years, as did the meals taken in it. The spacious and dignified dining room gave way to an alcove at one end of the living room or to a kitchen-dining room. Gateleg, drop-leaf and folding tables were very common because they could be tidied away to save space when not in use. Marian Speyer, a mid-1930s writer, commented in *Design for To-day* that

> …the starker modernists enjoy their calories in the ultra-hygienic surroundings of cellulose and glass…The disintegration has clearly set in. A few sensitised tablets taken in a couple of minutes may be all that is shortly left of the elaborate process once connected with dining and supping. The dining room may remain only as an historical memory.

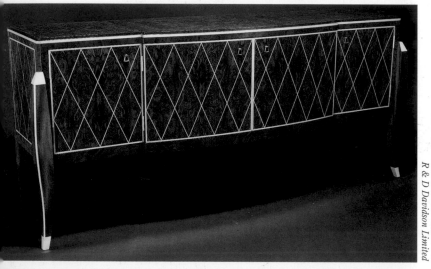

R & D Davidson Limited

R & D Davidson Limited

'Majik' brand dining tables could be extended when necessary with a gentle pull at each end to reveal two hidden leaves. The range also included sideboards, cupboards and service tables (which could also be used as writing desks). The last had a sliding top covering a partitioned cutlery and stationery tray, service extensions to the top and, at the ends, bookcases with hinged tray tops or revolving canteen cupboards. These items were made in various designs and sizes in oak, walnut or mahogany. The manufacturer also produced sectional bookcases, desks and easy chairs, so that the whole living room could be furnished with matching items.

An extending trestle dining table of the period, in figured walnut, paired well with small chairs with backs in figured walnut and loose seats covered in tapestry. The

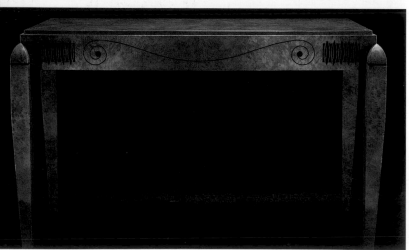

R & D Davidson Limited

THIS PAGE: *Dining rooms and furniture. This selection exemplifies the interesting range of styles to be found in interwar houses. At top left is a utilitarian room of simple design. The example at top right strikes a Tudor chord. The stylish dining suite at bottom, in chrome-plated metal and black-and-white lacquered wood, was designed by Marcel Breuer in 1926 – clearly for a select clientele.*

OPPOSITE: *A selection of tables, cabinets and chairs. The sideboard at centre left is a modern reproduction, very reminiscent of the piece designed by Ruhlmann in 1924 which is pictured on page 15.*

matching sideboard had chromium-plated handles. All three designs incorporated tapering steps. A luxury choice was an elegant, beech, D-ended table, standing on a double tripod. Another had a solid leg at each end, made of ebonized mahogany, and a contrasting surface of Japanese chestnut. The designer Duncan Miller created a dining table on three elephant-grey legs on cast-iron bases. Dining chairs of the period often had legs that splayed out at the back, giving the pieces something of the appearance of animals in lithe motion. An extravagant dining suite of the late 1930s consisted of an iron table with a top of black vitrolite on a silver base, and chairs with silver legs and covering of real zebra skin. Even inexpensive dining chairs were now being made to fit the occupant's back. Chromium-plated studs were available as a trim for furnishings such as dining chairs.

THIS PAGE AND OPPOSITE: *Dining furniture reflected Art Deco's preoccupation with classical or monumental shapes and exotic veneers.*

Living rooms

The term 'living room' began to be used in Britain only in the interwar years, having been promoted from the tenement dwelling to the middle- and upper-class vocabulary. Either term was used to designate an 'omnibus' room capable of serving many purposes: sitting room, dining room, playroom and study.

In general these rooms suffered with regard to comfort, and often efficiency, too, because people clung to their traditional fondness for single-purpose rooms. As a concession to flexibility and personal preferences, it was desirable that provision be made for screening off part of the room with curtains or folding doors. When designing a living room, owners were exhorted to treat the room as a complete entity from the outset. With the aid of modern methods, they could then achieve a room not 'lighted' and 'warmed' but 'in a state of being light and warm'.

In other countries the trend was towards open-plan living, with large, unpretentious rooms and enormous windows often extending the whole width of a room.

Furniture was typically kept 'close to the ground' in the late 1930s. Settees and armchairs were mostly built on geometrical, chunky lines, with low, wide, often square backs and armrests. Club chairs were made with

Rejuvenation Lamp and Fixture Co

removable seats and backs, stuffed with hair. The frames were of hardwood. A birch frame was used in some wing chairs. Swivel chairs with adjustable seats were comfortable items for office or study use. A modern piece was the divan, a backless settee or chaise longue. The Vienna divan curved upwards at both ends. An example designed by Betty Joel in about 1930 resembled a giant caterpillar, especially when covered in white silk velvet. In one version of this design, the upholstered seat rested on an ebony base.

Contrasting materials were much favoured for upholstery coverings: tapestry with velvet, for example.

THIS PAGE AND OPPOSITE: *Armchairs and settees were often very square, chunky and substantial, but wing chairs were also popular, and some seating was built-in.*

Upholstered furniture was customarily still provided with loose covers throughout the 1920s and 1930s, partly to provide some protection against coal dust. Flecked and striped fabrics were popular for these. For upholstery, 'real morocco' leather was an inexpensive option. In luxurious settings, sofas might be covered in silk satin or in moiré.

One design of occasional table consisted of a thick plate-glass rectangular top resting on a series of parallel S-shaped gold metal scrolls. Others were circular, decorated with crystal, silver plate, distressed mirror, Australian maple or sycamore. A more classical design was a rectangular table with a straight leg at each corner, made of rosewood and sycamore.

Every home supposedly had a use for the reversible table. One side of the top, in polished wood, was a coffee table; the other side, covered with baize, was a card table.

This page and opposite: Living-room seating of the 1930s was low and boxy. Upholstery fabric patterns were based on Cubist or Futurist designs in autumn colours. Tubular steel and light woods were fashionably modern.

LEFT: *Preliminary drawing for living room designed by R. W. Symonds in 1933. The glass column has light units at the top to reflect on to the ceiling for indirect lighting and they also reflect down on to the shelves and ornaments. At its base are three electric heating units which heat any part of the room required from the centre instead of from a fireplace. the furniture is in Nigerian cherry, a light-coloured wood new to furniture in this country.*

BELOW: *A bent plywood chair designed by The Makers of Simple furniture, London, in 1933, illustrating a very economical means of employing this material.*

ABOVE: *Living room in Dorset designed by Edward Maufe in 1933 to shift the emphasis from the fireplace to windows large and high enough to admit the maximum amount of sunlight.*

ABOVE: *Bentwood furniture from Finland - exhibited at Fortnums in London in 1934.*

R & D Davidson Limited

The tabletop could also be removed to serve as a tray or tilted vertically to act as a firescreen.

Folding flaps, either on bookcases or fixed directly to the wall, served as writing tables. The corner desk was another space-saving idea. Made of oak in any shade, it featured pigeonholes above the writing surface, a bookshelf on one side below and an extension shelf for a telephone. Roller or tambour doors were popular in cupboards and sideboards.

Bookcases were now being made to match other living-room furniture, such as desks, chairs and tables, or were sometimes built into the wall. To protect the books, some had a separate glass front to each shelf, either hinged to open outwards or unframed and sliding. Portable and extensible shelving was available, with adjustable shelves, to add capacity to existing bookcases.

Kidney-shaped knee-hole desks or writing tables were in fashion, echoing the style of the softly curved, feminine furniture exhibited by André Groult at the 1925 Paris Exposition, and using such materials as sycamore, gilt

bronze and glass. A partners' desk, made in 1930, was horizontally symmetrical with a kneehole and a set of drawers on each side so that partners could sit opposite each other. It came complete with two low armchairs.

THIS PAGE AND OPPOSITE: *Living-room furniture. The television and video cabinet shown this page, above left, is a modern reproduction of the 1920s works of master French*

Art Deco cabinetmakers such as Emile-Jacques Ruhlmann and Süe et Mare. On the opposite page, the armchair top right, the cupboard bottom left and the table bottom centre are also reproductions.

Bedrooms

Decorative schemes for bedrooms usually consisted of muted colours but offered some contrasts. Against a backdrop of pale cream walls, doors and furniture might be painted in a delicate blue-green and complemented by a mauve carpet and chintz bedspreads. In the ordinary home, furniture was very simple, the principal form being the plain rectangle. Legs were carved into spindle shapes, but without further surface ornament.

Louis Sognot (1892–1970), a French Modernist furniture designer, created the bedroom furniture for the palace of the Maharajah of Indore in 1930, which was built and decorated by the German architect Eckart Muthesius. The pale green bed and the lavish headboard featured double glass shelves at each side which were decorated with chromium bands.

A typical bedroom suite for a suburban interwar house consisted of a wardrobe, a seven-drawer dressing table with triple frameless mirrors, a fitted tallboy with drawers and mirror, and a bed with an interior-sprung mattress. Figured walnut was the most popular material for this ensemble, but some suites were also made in oak. By the 1930s, the divan bed was becoming so popular that almost half the beds sold were of that type. They had detachable padded and covered headboards, which could be matched to the colour scheme of the room and re-covered when that scheme came up for replacement.

According to the Seng Company of Chicago, the 'world's largest makers of furniture hardware', ordinary wooden beds creaked and squeaked and were subject to distortion, while metal beds were 'inartistic'. The company's 'Seng-equipt Beds of Wood', by contrast, combined wood for beauty and steel for strength – 'the advantages of both and the demerits of neither'. The steel frame was clothed in a wooden exterior. This kind of bed was hygienic and 'silent as the stars'.

The dressing table underwent a transformation when armour-plate glass began to be used for the actual table. The mirror was usually of cheval-glass length, although circular mirrors were equally popular. A touch of luxury was provided by the addition of a padded footrest. A piece of furniture called a 'coiffeuse' was a simplified dressing table with a central section topped by a hinged lid that opened up to reveal a mirror. One example, made by the Société Industrielle d'Art of Paris, was in metal and mirror glass. Its interior was lined with white kid and a matching stool was similarly upholstered.

Round mirrors were symptomatic of a trend towards curves. In this, the British stole a march on the normally advanced French, anticipating the demand for items that

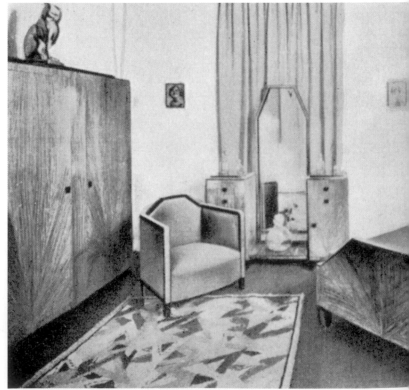

The Seymour

FIGURED WALNUT BEDROOM SUITE

This Bedstead is made either as a double or single

THE DARK MOCCASA EBONY VENEERS FORM AN INTERESTING CONTRAST TO THE LIGHTER WALNUT FINISH

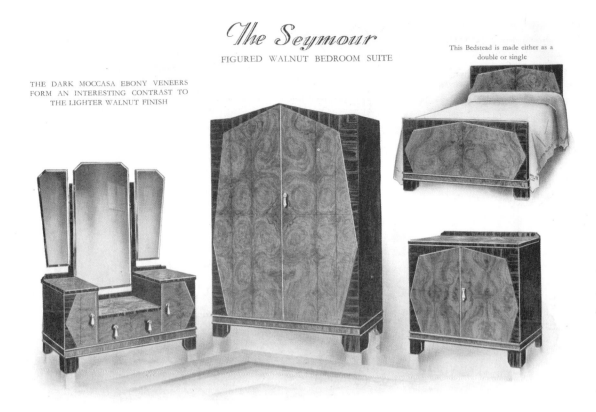

THIS PAGE AND OPPOSITE: *Most of these pictures of bedroom furniture are taken from contemporary catalogues and illustrate the popular usage of dark and light woods as a design feature for bedroom suites, as in Art Deco furniture in general.*

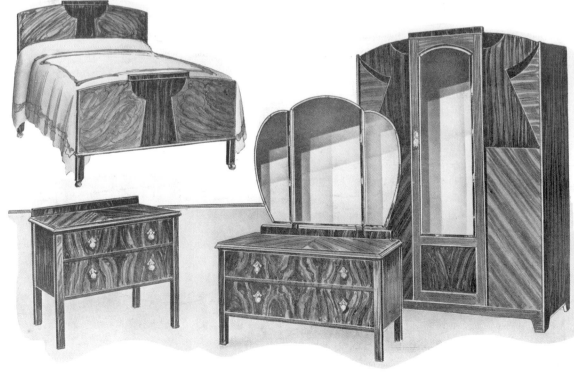

LITLUX

The Non-glare Bed Light

The pendant shades shown with the Litlux have a patent fixing attachment by which the shade is automatically held in position by the electric lamp. No screwing, no straining.

LL 1110.—Double Soft Silk, covered hand painted tapestry design, Silk Tassels.

48/-

Pendant Shade to match. 6" extreme, 35/-

LL 1078.—Imitation Vellum, beautifully hand-painted in oils.

27/-

Pendant Shade to match. 6" dia. 9/-

LL 1111.—Double Soft Silk, covered Georgette, floral trimming.

37/6

Pendant Shade to match, 5" dia. 15/-

not only were but also looked more comfortable. The new 'rounded' armchairs were ultra-wide and deep. A novelty was the chair that lacked any kind of steel or linen webbing, becoming a kind of floating platform that was marvellously comfortable. In an elaborately furnished bedroom, stools or chairs might be upholstered in buttoned velvet, and buttoned or quilted satin might cover the headboard or form the drapes around a dressing table.

A device popular in the USA was the fold-away bed. A metal bedstead swivelled round an adjacent doorway into the dressing room, where it folded into a recess during the day. The disadvantage of this arrangement was the cumbersome metal chassis, which was decidedly unsightly.

Well-to-do householders might have separate day and night nurseries for a baby. The day nursery also served as a playroom and therefore called for scrupulous cleanliness and good ventilation. Linoleum was the recommended floor covering, being so easy to clean; the more smooth-surfaced and plainer the better, because that immediately revealed any speck of dirt to the meticulously hygienic mother. In winter, a rug provided a warmer surface to sit on. Rubber sheeting, oil-silk or American cloth – fabrics that were then popular for bathrooms and kitchens – were also recommended for nursery curtains because they could be wiped clean. Simple coarse linens were an alternative.

Washable wallpaper or varnished distemper were good wall treatments for similar reasons. On the walls, appliqué motifs could be placed to create a recurring pattern or a continuous frieze. A large panel of black linoleum fixed to a wall could serve as a drawing board (for use with chalk).

All in the Past

THIS PAGE AND OPPOSITE:
Bedrooms displayed a huge
variety of styles, some highly
ornate, others pared down to
the bare functional minimum.

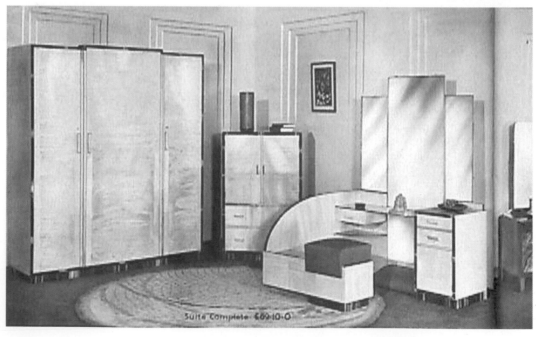

Suite Complete: £69·10·0

THIS PAGE AND OPPOSITE: *Many of the interiors here represent what was thought to be the best in contemporary design.*

Kitchens

In the kitchen, plain whitewood furniture was coming to the fore, having the advantage that it looked naturally clean and hygienic and could be rendered more so by scrubbing with disinfectant soap. Built-in cupboards replaced shelved dressers, as they were easier to clean and took up less space in the new smaller kitchen or kitchenette. Sink units were available made from silver-coloured Monel metal. They were strong and absolutely rustless.

Porcelain enamel on work tables, cookers, washers and wringers proved a boon to householders because it was easy to clean. Galvanized iron was also good for washers, but less easily cleanable. Aluminium cooking utensils were coming into use during the interwar years. They were advertised as attractive and durable, offering fuel savings because they conducted heat well.

The Kernerator was an incinerator built into the base of the chimney when the house was erected. It was made to burn all refuse including cans and bottles and required no fuel other than the dry waste that burnt the wet waste.

The water softener worked on the base-exchange principle. Calcium and magnesium salts passing through the softener reacted with the softening materials and were converted into completely soluble sodium salts. New to the market in 1934 was a baby water softener, which was about the size and shape of a modern electric kettle. Made of white earthenware with chromium fittings, it was portable and connected easily to a tap, making it ideal for a bathroom or kitchen.

Like its British counterpart, the typical Australian kitchen between the wars was servantless. Its equipment and fittings included a gas stove, an enamel-topped table, an ice chest, a storage safe and a porcelain sink (perhaps in an adjoining scullery). The floor was covered with linoleum, probably blue and white. Whereas the all-electric home had become commonplace in Europe and America in the 1910s, Australia lagged behind. People thought electricity was expensive and accordingly gas reigned supreme for lighting and cooking. But there was no denying the inevitable; by 1915 it was clear that electricity had a great future.

The first domestic refrigerators had appeared in 1913 and 60 per cent of the US population owned one by 1941. The early models were simply metal cabinets housing a relatively large motor and rather little storage space. Raymond Loewy designed the Coldspot Super Six refrigerator for the US mail order firm Sears Roebuck around 1934. Its pressed-steel frame was reminiscent of car bodywork, with rounded corners and a gleaming white finish. Electrolux refrigerators now had ten-way

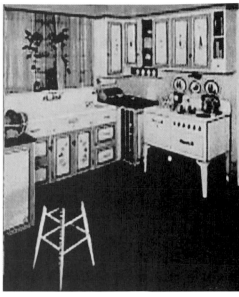

THIS PAGE AND OPPOSITE: *Kitchens often doubled as eating rooms. Built-in furniture was becoming common and electric appliances were finding their way into suburban kitchens. Cookers tended to be large items, capable of performing a range of duties, including central heating.*

temperature control, were air-cooled, motorless and operated silently and automatically by gas, electricity or paraffin. Refrigerators were often thought unnecessary however, especially in Britain, because the housewife, having no other calls on her time and living close to the shops, could readily buy what she needed every day.

The Aga was invented by Gustaf Dalen, a Swedish Nobel Prize winner, in 1922, and it was licensed for production in Britain in 1929. The inventor's only lapse – in modern eyes – was his choice of asbestos as an insulating material. It immediately became a great and enduring success. As Aga owners of the twenty-first century know, this cooker lived up to the advertising description of it as 'a profitable investment'. An Aga cost 59 guineas (£61.95) plus a small charge for delivery and installation; as much as the complete furnishings of a main bedroom, but it eventually paid for itself in lower fuel costs. It consumed no more than £4 worth of anthracite or coke a year, even

though it burnt night and day and irrespective of how much it was used or how many people it served. It was easy to clean, having chromium-plated exterior metal parts and glazed, non-cracking, vitreous enamel sides, back, front and top plates.

The Aga comprised a boiling plate and a simmering plate, each with an insulating lid to be shut down to prevent loss of heat when the plates were not in use; a roasting oven; a large, slow-cooking oven in which dishes could safely be left to cook unattended, even overnight; and an inside cooking tank containing 10 gallons (45 litres) of water just off the boil – handy for quick boiling of vegetables, washing up and instantaneous filling of hot-water bottles. Draught was controlled by a thermostat and no flames came into contact with cooking utensils, which meant that these did not become dirty on the outside.

At the other end of the size scale from the Aga was the 'Kubex' electric oven, a small, self-contained unit that could

Kitchen furniture and appliances. Refrigerators were coming into general use only slowly in the 1920s and 1930s, although these appliances now had some sophisticated features. the Kitchen cabinet, right, made of oak, was considered the latest in kitchen equipment. The top section contained

'6 gilt hilt canisters for tea, coffee, etc, metal flour bin with sifting device, egg rack, rack on door containing 5 spice jars, memory tickler, and rack for tradesmen's books, etc'. The bottom was fitted with a table of white vitreous porcelain enamel which slid away when not in use, and a meat safe.

be used in any room, connected to any lighting or power socket. The oven could be used to cook for a family of four or as an auxiliary to the cooker in regular use. A heat regulator was fixed at one side, and there was also a grill.

The new gas stoves had armour-plate, fireproof, non-steaming and practically unbreakable glass doors. They were finished inside and out with porcelain enamel, which was easy to clean. A splash-back, eye-level plate-warming rack and a chromium-plated towel rail were fitted. The 'Regulo' thermostatic control was developed for gas stoves in 1923. This freed the cook from the constant need to check the temperature of the oven. An ignition lighter also dispensed with the need for matches to light the burners. Gas cookers had the further advantage that they were cheaper than electric models. The 'Double Sterling' oven, manufactured by the Sill Stove Works of Rochester, New York, from 1849, boasted two ovens, each large enough for the biggest turkey, side by side on the same level, and a very large top surface

fuelled by gas and coal, all on one level, such that nine utensils could be used at one time. The complete range was 49 inches (124 centimetres) wide and its polished top required 'no blacking'. In reality, solid fuel ranges, used for cooking and for heating water and air, required a lot of refuelling and cleaning and in the summer a fire still had to be lit to provide hot water and for cooking.

Another model of cooker, made by Bramhall, Deane Company of New York City, burnt coal and wood in one section and gas in the oven. The fire would start quickly and heat was readily retained in the oven. The gas section had large and medium-sized burners, a large oven and a shelf for open-fire roasting and toasting. The range was made of rust-resistant iron with polished-steel trimmings.

Innovations to cookers in the 1930s included a hinged cover which folded down to conceal the top of the cooker and the taps, and a stand, which obviated the kneeling and stooping required with older cookers.

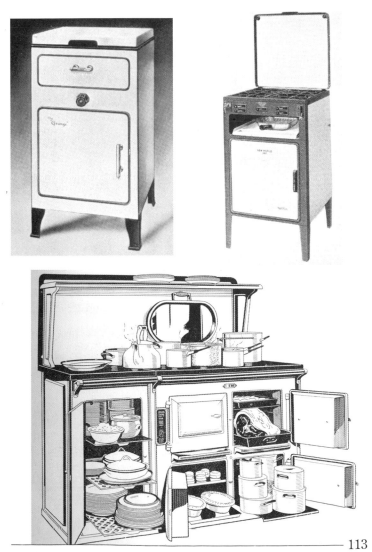

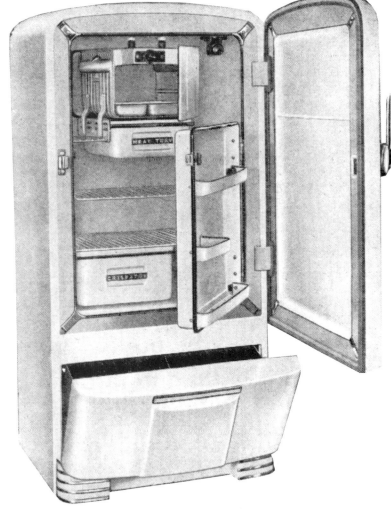

The bathroom

The functionalism of Modernist design translated easily into the style of the average bathroom. Even in British suburban houses built in mock-Tudor style, the bathroom was usually fitted in an up-to-date fashion.

Tiles – sometimes hand-decorated – were considered ideal for the walls, at least up to dado height. Baths were boxed in and fitted with chromium-plated taps, possibly with a shower attachment. Pedestal wash-basins and toilets were made in streamlined shapes. One porcelain basin,

H & R Johnson Tiles Limited

H & R Johnson Tiles Limited

THIS PAGE AND OPPOSITE: *In the 1930s a bathroom could be a bare, cold place from which to make the quickest possible escape or a luxury room fitted out in palatial splendour. Glass and marble were used extensively and created a feeling of opulence.*

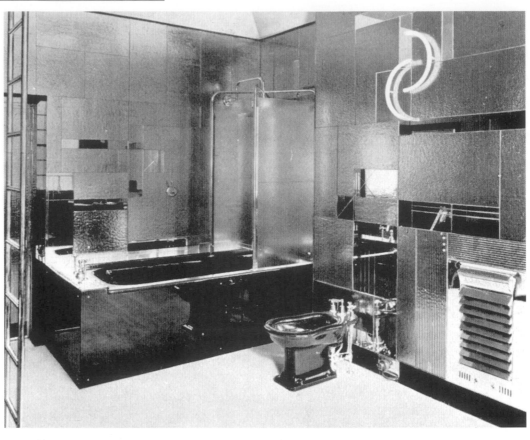

THIS PAGE AND OPPOSITE: *Glass was a popular feature in interwar bathrooms, especially in wealthier homes. Tiled walls and the high-level flush toilet were typically found in the bathroom of an ordinary suburban house.*

designed in France by Jacob Delphon in the 1920s, was octagonal in shape and was one of the first to use colour-coding to distinguish hot and cold taps. It is still in production. A new feature in toilets was the silent flush, as the old high-level cistern was gradually replaced by a low-level version and eventually by the quieter syphonic closet.

The en-suite bathroom was already a feature of some houses in the 1930s. One option was to have double doors between the bedroom and bathroom, which could be folded back against the walls. In the most luxurious bathrooms, the floor might be raised to give the effect of a sunken bath, or the bath set, Hollywood-style, in a wide raised marble platform. Bathroom cabinets and furniture featured white finishes, mirrors and chromium-plated fittings. Chromium-plated towel rails were heated by connecting them to the hot-water system.

'The spiritual home of glass, of course,' wrote Edward Crankshaw (in *Design for To-day*, October 1934), 'is the bathroom. Ours is pre-eminently an age of plumbing, and the conservative British generally go modern from the bathroom outwards.' By this token it was possible to have plate-glass shelves, glass towel rails, translucent glass walls illuminated from behind; even, at a pinch, a bath of transparent moulded glass.

Chapter 4
Furnishings &
Interior Decoration

One can furnish a room very luxuriously by taking out furniture
rather than putting it in.

Francis Jourdain

Sarah Gallaher, Period House Magazine

Tr ue Art Deco furniture now fetches high prices because of its rarity and because it represents the value of quality craftsmanship, a dying art. Experts have argued therefore that the furniture, more than any other expression of Art Deco style, deserves preservation.

As Arie van de Lemme has pointed out in *The Encyclopedia of Decorative Styles 1850–1935*, there were two distinct trends within Art Deco furniture design. On the one hand, there were early experiments in modern furniture, using metals and plastics in forms that could lead to mass production. On the other, there was the high-quality craftsmanship destined for an exclusive market. In the eyes of purists, only the latter category qualifies as Art Deco furniture. The battle between the traditionalists and the Modernists lasted only as long as the heyday of Art Deco, which managed for a short time to contain the opposing forces. In the end it was the Modernists who won.

Traditionalists in France aimed to produce highly refined pieces of furniture by applying perfect techniques to the finest and most exotic materials. André Mare (1887–1932) founded the Compagnie des Arts Français in 1919 with Louis Süe, in reaction to the more 'monstrous' extensions of an otherwise 'sane' art – Art Nouveau. With their colleagues André Groult, Clément Mère, Paul Follot and Emile-Jacques Ruhlmann, Süe et Mare became the exemplars and leaders of the Art Deco movement in France. Their furniture characteristically displayed a predilection for curves, wood contrasts, carved details and lacquers. They used woods such as mahogany, macassar ebony (from South-east Asia), violet wood, rosewood,

BELOW: *This stylized fountain design forms a pair of cabinet handles in birch and vavona wood with bas-relief bronze.*

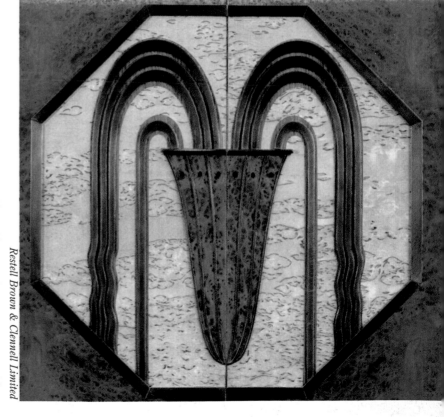

Restell Brown & Clennell Limited

OPPOSITE: *Jagged edges and sharp points contrasting with a scallop-rimmed bowl make a striking ceiling light for a living room.*

sycamore and elm. The interior decorator Jules Leleu was especially fond of a rosewood called palisander. Other materials that were highly favoured included sharkskin, shagreen, tortoiseshell, mother-of-pearl, ivory, glass and lacquer; and metals such as gold, silver, iron, copper and aluminium. Very careful finishes, fine surface treatments and sensitive control of materials were the hallmarks of Art Deco furniture. There was no symbolism, nor were any purely accidental surface inequalities allowed to create haphazard effects of light and shade.

Emile-Jacques Ruhlmann (1879–1933) was the greatest exponent of this style of furniture. He was born in Paris and inherited his father's building and decorating firm in 1907. He exhibited furniture designs at the Salon d'Automne from 1913 onwards. After World War I, he set up a large furniture workshop, Etablissements Ruhlmann et Laurent, which became the most prestigious decorating firm in France. He achieved a great triumph with his furniture for the Hôtel du Collectioneur at the Paris Exposition in 1925. Ruhlmann made unconstrained use of mahogany, macassar ebony, amboyna and inlaid ivory or tortoiseshell. His designs for the Maharajah of Indore included a spectacular polished-metal bed. His furniture took Art Deco style to its opulent extreme and was consequently never put into industrial production.

The influence of the elite furniture makers spread widely, however. Design became a buzzword, particularly in the 1930s, and the new department stores realized that by incorporating 'design' into their goods they could reach a large market. Equally, customers were pleased to be able to buy the most modern furniture at reasonable prices.

Mahogany, having fallen out of favour, returned in the 1930s to dining rooms and, in a light-coloured form, to bedrooms. It was polished to a coral pink and other attractive colours. For bedrooms, the trend was towards lightness, for which light walnut, both straight-grained and figured, Indian greywood, Indian laurel and Australian walnut were suitable. Macassar ebony and sycamore also played a part. Canadian flame birch was an attractive wood that was introduced into Britain only in the mid-1930s. Mountain ash made a nice contrast in furniture of English grey walnut, or on its own. It was also used for floors. Most of these woods could be left plain, decorated in flower designs or painted.

Modernism and new materials

Innovators of the period preferred to simplify the lines and decoration of their furniture. A few continued to use traditional materials such as leather and fine woods, but most used metal, especially hollow metal tubing, which could be painted. Such pieces also lent themselves to mass production. In his last few years Ruhlmann himself made some concessions to Modernism, using elements such as chromium, tubular steel and black lacquer to make, for example, a chromium-plated metal lamp and a kidney-shaped desk with telephone fitment.

Chromium is a brilliant, silvery, metallic element obtained by smelting from chrome ironstone. It is resistant

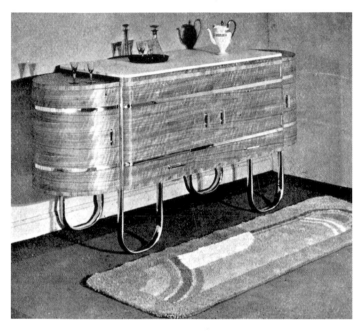

ABOVE: *Chromium, tubular steel, inlaid wood and glass are all combined in this sideboard.*

OPPOSITE, FAR LEFT: *A cabinet in cherry wood by Gordon Russell was on show at the Third Annual Exhibition of work by Cotswold artists in the summer of 1934.*

OPPOSITE, LEFT, AND RIGHT: *Occasional tables in futuristic designs were made of the most modern materials – glass and tubular steel.*

to corrosion. Though it had been discovered in 1798, it did not become commercially available until 1925, when designers were quick to appreciate its suitability as a finish for tubular steel. Developed in Germany under a process patented in 1885, tubular steel was characterized by the absence of any visible seam along its length. Its use increased greatly in the 1920s when it was seized upon by Modernist furniture designers interested in the possibilities of mass production.

Mart Stam (1899–1986), who had practised as an architect in his native Netherlands and in Germany and Switzerland and had also worked as a town planner in the Soviet Union, designed the first tubular-steel cantilevered chair in 1926. Marcel Breuer and Ludwig Mies van der Rohe also produced tubular-steel chairs which are now considered classics of twentieth-century furniture design. Finished with chromium, tubular-steel furniture represented the very essence of Modernism.

The Thonet furniture company had been founded in 1853 by Michael Thonet (1796–1871) who, far ahead of his time, developed the bentwood chair. Some of the company's timeless designs were used by Le Corbusier to furnish his Esprit Nouveau pavilion at the 1925 Exposition and, by 1930, some fifty million of the company's bentwood Chair No. 14 had been produced in its factories scattered over central Europe. From the 1920s, it also produced tubular-steel furniture. Another pioneer in chair-making was Gerald Summers (1899–1967), who designed plywood furniture, including a lounge chair made from a single piece of plywood.

Ambrose Heal (1872–1959) was the leading light in the family firm of Heal's in London, of which he became chairman in 1913. Heal also helped to found the Design and Industries Association in 1915. Under him, the furniture manufactured and retailed by Heal's became simpler and starker, moving towards Modernism in the 1930s with designs that made use of tubular steel and laminated woods. Having begun work in the Arts and Crafts genre, the British furniture designer and craftsman Gordon Russell (1892–1980) also absorbed the ideas of Modernism. He exhibited at the Paris Exposition of 1925. The furniture designs of Lucie Renaudot, who was active during the 1930s, were conceived on very simple, almost classical lines, although they were not as free of decoration as contemporary furniture produced in Britain.

Woven-fibre furniture was durable and attractive, with figured effects and charming colours. The Lloyd Loom company was established to produce an imitation wicker made from twisted craft paper fibre strengthened with wire, invented by the American Marshall Lloyd (1858–1927).

This material was used to create inexpensive chairs, chests and other furniture, which became very popular in the interwar years.

Another new material, Bakelite, was named for its inventor, the Belgian-born chemist Leo H. Baekeland. It is a thermosetting plastic of brittle texture, usually reinforced with a filler of fibre and wood flour. It was first used in the electrical industry, but its cheapness and resemblance to wood made it ideal for mass-market products such as telephones and radios. Its modernity appealed greatly to the newly technologically aware public of the 1920s and 1930s.

Glass

Originally a successful jeweller, René Lalique (1860–1945) began using glass in his jewellery designs, and eventually abandoned his first career to concentrate on glass design. In 1909 he established Cristal Lalique, and the title of principal designer passed, on his death, to his son and then (in 1977) to his granddaughter. Flowers and fruit were favourite motifs and he also produced an exquisite set of luminaires (panels and sculpted pieces lit from inside their bases), which were decorated with peacocks,

which he designed many successful pieces himself using coloured art glass. These were based on the French Art Deco style, as for example his series of hunting-design vases (made around 1925), which featured leaping gazelles, stylized foliage, curves and zigzags.

Glass was immensely popular in 1930s interiors, used abundantly for tabletops, light fittings, candleholders and mirrors. Armour-plate glass was a novelty, and was virtually unbreakable and absolutely transparent. The only proviso was that the glass had to be cut and shaped before being armour-plated, after which it could not be tampered with further. Anything could be made of it: bookshelves, trays, tabletops, whole tables, desks and chairs. Sink splashbacks were sometimes formed of safety glass made by rolling two or more sheets of white, non-splintering glass on to a cellulosed backing.

A semi-transparent, heavy moulded glass was used for items such as ashtrays and light fittings. In conjunction with reinforced concrete it was used architecturally in the construction of skylights and pavement lights.

A type of glass alloy called 'vitrolite' was important in interior decoration. It was generally made in flat panels of varying sizes, to be used plain, etched or sandblasted for

FAR LEFT: *Two samples of pottery by the British designer Clarice Cliff.*

LEFT: *Vase designed by Frederick Carder for the Steuben Glass Company, made from blue aurene over jade yellow glass, 1920s.*

swallows and knights in armour. Eventually, his repertoire extended to mirrors, tables and architectural fittings: for the first-class dining saloon on the liner *Normandie*, he designed a spectacular illuminated glass ceiling, wall panels and chandeliers.

Frederick Carder (1863–1963), a British émigré to the USA, co-founded the Steuben Glassworks in New York (1903), which was taken over by the Corning Glass Works in 1918. He was art director there for 30 years, during

decorative use. Sandblasting, then a new process, gave an extraordinarily complete illusion of relief engraving. Another method of turning glass into a ground for decorative design was etching with acid and then painting, which produced a kind of modern fresco. Back-lit or mirrored glass was used as panelling on interior walls, mainly in public buildings such as hotels and theatres. Rose-tinted mirrors were flattering and popular features of 1930s fireplace surrounds.

Ceramics

Clarice Cliff (1899–1972), one of the most important British ceramic designers of the period, specialized in household pottery in strikingly bold, brightly coloured, stylized designs that typified Art Deco. Her best-known work was the Bizarre range, created in 1928, which was extremely unusual for its striking, almost garish decoration applied in big blocks of colour, and its geometric shapes. She spent most of her working life within the company of Newport Wilkinson, achieving her greatest successes with her hand-painted ceramics. In 1932, she also used contemporary artists, including Graham Sutherland, Vanessa Bell and Laura Knight, as designers and exhibited the resulting range at Harrods in London, though it was not well received.

Cliff's contemporary Susie Cooper (1902–95), another British ceramicist, produced domestic ware fashioned in strong, simple shapes and muted tones, often with a natural theme. Her trademark motif was a leaping deer. Cooper's success derived from her design and marketing skills and her respect for British taste: the 'Jazz style' decorative schemes she adopted, though usually abstract and geometrical, were pleasingly subdued.

Edvard Hald (1883–1980), a Swedish glassmaker and ceramicist, was associated with the Swedish glassworks Orrefors from 1917 until his death, and served as its managing director for a time, though he designed porcelain for other makers. He won a grand prize at the Paris Exposition. His work showed both Swedish modern and traditional features. The early work of the Hungarian ceramicist Eva Zeisel (born 1906) conformed with the vogue for geometric patterns. After moving to the USA in 1938, she also began to work in the Modernist genre.

ABOVE LEFT: *A Lloyd Loom suite, made from twisted paper.*

ABOVE: *Chair and stool of chrome-plated steel and leather by Mies van der Rohe, 1929.*

LEFT: *Chair by Francis Jourdain, 1925. The seat and back are of wickerwork.*

BELOW: *White lead and lacquer veneers decorate this armchair by Marcel Coard, early 1920s.*

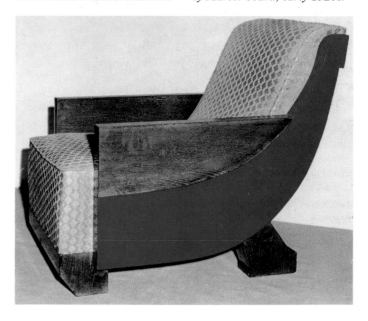

Metals and metal wares

Art Deco metalwork was highly inventive and adaptable. In the 1920s wrought iron, copper and bronze were the materials of choice. Wrought iron could be used for pieces as small as a mantelpiece clock or as large as the entrance gates for the Paris Exposition of 1925. There was a continuing vogue for wrought iron in furniture, partly arising from the fact that certain shapes – such as curved and scrolled table bases – could not be made satisfactorily in any other material. Its most gifted exponent was probably Edgar Brandt (1880–1960), who usually worked to commissions from architects, designing not only large items such as monumental doors or staircases – not least for the ocean liners *Paris*, *Ile de France* and *Normandie* – but also ordinary domestic objects including ceiling light fittings and sconces, vases, bowls, table lamps, radiator covers, firescreens, mirror frames and console tables. He exhibited at the annual Paris Salons and won the commission to design the Paris Exposition's imposing Gate of Honour. His output was vast; he also occasionally worked in bronze, gilt-copper, steel or aluminium, and created lampshades in alabaster, often for the firm of Daum Frères.

Brandt's contemporary, the furniture designer Armand Albert Rateau (1882–1938), produced some nicely eccentric metal pieces, including a bronze chaise longue that rested on the backs of four bronze deer. Raymond Henri Subes (1893–1970) was another major exponent of decorative forged ironwork, which often featured lively motifs such as stylized roses and arabesques. He was responsible for a range of architectural commissions in the 1920s, such as churches, monuments and hotels, and for some magnificent work on both the façades and interiors of Art Deco buildings.

Traditional materials were not forgotten in the 1930s, but designers were beginning to favour the more modern aluminium, steel and chrome, used in their starkest, most unadorned manifestations. Shiny metals were favoured for their qualities of reflectivity and brilliance.

The Danish silversmith Georg Jensen (1866–1935) was described by the *New York Daily Herald* as 'the greatest craftsman in silver of the last three hundred years'. He founded the silver company Jensen and designed many of the pieces it produced, particularly in the interwar years, including jewellery, candlesticks, coffee and tea services and other fine domestic wares. His collaborator was the painter Johan Rohde (1856–1935). The company made handcrafted silver in a restrained Modernist genre at reasonable prices and thus became very successful. Jean Puiforçat (1897–1945) was another outstanding silversmith, who has a claim to be regarded as the founder of modern silverwork. Having studied in London, he founded a workshop in 1921. His silverware had clean lines and smooth surfaces. In pursuit of functionality, he concentrated essentially on three shapes – the sphere, the cone and the cylinder – and his pieces were characterized by simple geometry and perfect proportions. He occasionally combined silver with contrasting materials such as semi-precious stones and rare woods. His work was very precise, in a style sometimes described as 'Cubist' but which he termed 'mathematical'. It represented a new architectural approach that departed from the exaltation of surface decoration typical of traditional silverwork.

Emile-Jacques Ruhlmann and René Lalique were also practitioners of the Art Deco style in silverware. Lalique had his own pavilion at the Paris Exposition in 1925, and

BELOW: *A three-panel screen by one of America's most influential Art Deco designers, Donald Deskey, 1929.*

also designed and manufactured furniture for the Sèvres porcelain factory pavilion. He had trained as a goldsmith in France and England and in the mid-1880s began to build up a jewellery manufacturing firm. He achieved great success among the wealthy elite, for whom he made jewellery, glass ornaments and later also textiles and mirrors, in designs that incorporated symbolist with classical and oriental sources.

In America, the Chase Brass and Copper Company was the most successful producer of chrome and nickel utensils and accessories in the 1930s. A typical example of their output is a pair of 'Bubble' candlesticks: each features a chromium-plated sphere resting on a dark blue glass square which is mounted on a chromium base.

Interior designers

Like other furniture designers of the period, Ruhlmann was an *ensemblier*: he created a room's entire decorative scheme, designing not only furniture – with his hallmark slender, tapered legs – but also carpets, fabrics and lighting. Eileen Gray (1879–1976) also worked primarily in the Art Deco style, although she herself vigorously rejected the epithet when it was later coined. She was famous for her technically sophisticated lacquer screens of the 1920s, and for other furniture designs, notably in aluminium and glass. Irish-born, she studied drawing and lacquerwork in London and in Paris, where she worked with a Japanese lacquerworker and cabinetmaker, Seizo Sugawara. From 1922 she sold her furniture and textile designs from her own workshop and shop, and after 1926

she worked on architectural projects with Jean Badovici, for whom she designed a house. Recognizing that she and her contemporaries lived 'in an incredibly outdated environment', she set out to 'make things for our time'. As time went on her style became closer to that of Le Corbusier and the Modernists and she began to use less lacquer and more chromed tubular steel and aluminium. After 1930 her furniture incorporated more novelties and gadgets, such as cabinets with pivoting drawers. Her carpets, often featuring crisp, angular designs, contrasted with and softened the austerity of her interiors.

ABOVE: *Victoire, a moulded glass car mascot by René Lalique, c. 1930.*

LEFT: *An interior grille by Edgar Brandt.*

Sugawara also trained Jean Dunand (1877–1942), a Swiss best known for his lacquerwork and a master of *dinanderie* (work in non-precious metals). He frequently combined lacquer with metal to make such objects as furniture, screens and panels, often engraved or sculpted and decorated with encrustations of mother-of-pearl or crushed eggshell. Some of his best-known work graced the interiors of Art Deco structures, including the ocean liner *Normandie* (1935). Dunand also produced sculptures and his later style was intensely eclectic, embracing African and Oriental figures, landscapes, flowers, fish and birds.

Donald Deskey (1894–1989) was one of the most influential Art Deco designers in the USA during the 1930s, working with new materials such as aluminium, cork and linoleum. From highly practical items such as washing machines and printing presses, he moved on to design interiors, including wallpapers, carpets and fabrics, preferring asymmetrical geometric forms. He excelled in metalwork, using aluminium and polished chrome to great

effect in luxury furnishings; and made use of glass both in exteriors – as glass bricks to create indirect lighting – and in furniture, in the form of glass tabletops and shelves. Deskey's classic Radio City Music Hall interior in New York City is a supreme example of Art Deco design.

The French fashion designer Paul Poiret (1879–1944) set up his own salon in 1904, in which he promoted designs with a distinct oriental flavour. In 1911 he founded L'Ecole Martine, a school of decorative arts for girls, whose nature drawings formed the basis for a wide range of exotic designs for textiles. Output from the school included carpets, pianos, lampshades, cushions, chairs, sofas, beds and tables. For the 1925 Paris Exposition, Poiret created an exhibit consisting of three flower-painted barges, fitted out with wall hangings and other interior furnishings, moored beneath the Alexandre III bridge. Poiret's clothing designs – some Eastern-inspired, others long, tubular and unornamented – were in perfect step with the Art Deco age and exerted an influence far beyond the area of couture.

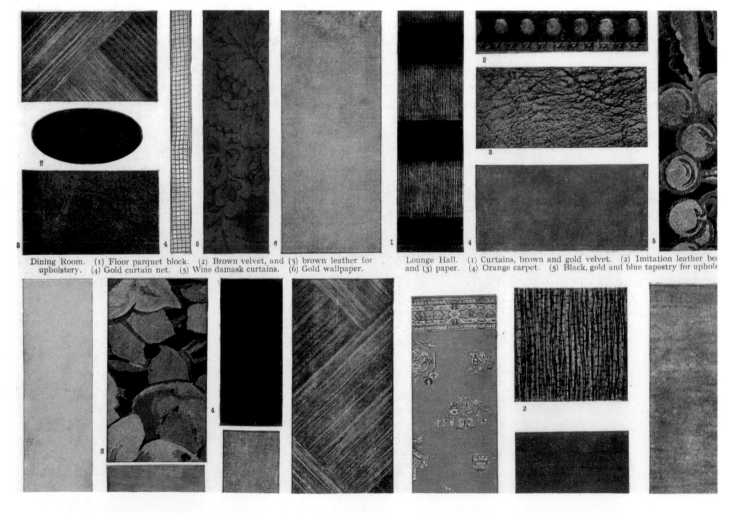

Dining Room. (1) Floor parquet block. (2) Brown velvet, and (3) brown leather for upholstery. (4) Gold curtain net. (5) Wine damask curtains. (6) Gold wallpaper.

Lounge Hall. (1) Curtains, brown and gold velvet. (2) Imitation leather bea and (3) paper. (4) Orange carpet. (5) Black, gold and blue tapestry for uphols

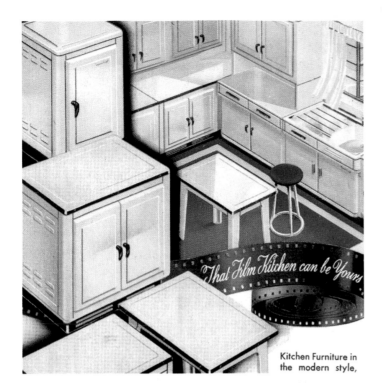

Kitchen Furniture in
the modern style,

Art Deco in the suburban home

Even though Modernist architecture was generally rejected in the suburbs in favour of more traditional styles, the influence of contemporary designers found its way into most homes in the interwar period in the form of objects – from dressing tables to ashtrays – and interior decoration. Preoccupations with sunshine, fresh air and hygiene led to lighter colour schemes and less cluttered interiors, while new electric light fittings and kitchen gadgetry injected the streamlined styling of the machine age.

Ivory, terracotta, coral, emerald green, celadon green and geranium red were among the most popular colours in interwar houses. A bedroom designed by Derek Patmore around 1937 was called the 'Renoir' bedroom because its colour scheme made use of three tones often used by the painter: subtle sage green, soft grey blue and cerise red. By the mid-1930s, colour codification had been adopted in certain branches of the textile industry, but not in other branches of interior decoration, such as paint colours. An exception was an initial dozen shades which were standardized by the British Colour Council for vitreous-enamelled domestic appliances.

ABOVE AND RIGHT: *White was the favourite colour for kitchen furniture, being clean-looking and a suitable backdrop for the display of kitchenware and ornaments.*

OPPOSITE: *Colour schemes from* The Concise Household Encyclopedia *(1931): dining room (top left), lounge hall (top right), sitting room (bottom left), bedroom (bottom right). The schemes contain suggestions for flooring, wallpaper, curtains, carpets, upholstery and woodwork.*

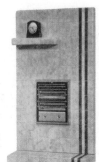

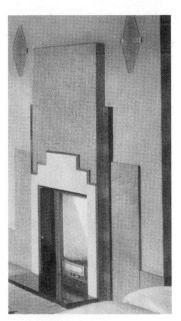

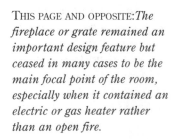

THIS PAGE AND OPPOSITE: *The fireplace or grate remained an important design feature but ceased in many cases to be the main focal point of the room, especially when it contained an electric or gas heater rather than an open fire.*

In kitchens, white was thought the best background against which to see whether china, glass and crockery had been properly washed. The whitewood looked clean and hygienic and could be kept so by scrubbing with disinfectant soap.

Fireplaces

In most suburban houses of the period – except for those which, in Moderne style, omitted chimneys altogether – a fireplace was still an essential feature of the reception rooms, and fireplaces were also provided upstairs where chimneys passed through the bedrooms. However, open fires were rarely lit except in living rooms, and began to be replaced by gas or electric fittings. Another alternative was solid-fuel stoves, which could in some cases be installed in existing fireplaces. These would burn continuously throughout the winter and were advertised as needing no attention for ten or twelve hours at a time. They consumed ordinary coal, coke or anthracite and were obtainable in various designs and sizes and in coloured enamel finishes. Anthracite stoves could provide continuous 'central heating'. Coke fires burned with a smokeless blaze, increasing heating capacity, reducing fuel costs, preserving the interior decorations and eliminating the need to sweep the chimney.

Brick and tile fireplace surrounds were both popular, as were mirror glass panels. Rose tinted mirror was a contemporary touch in 1938.

Petra Hellas

Olde Englande Reproductions

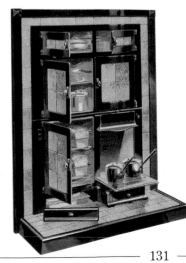

THIS PAGE AND OPPOSITE: *A selection of fireplaces and grates in brick, marble and ironwork.*

Floor coverings

During the interwar period, fitted carpets were expensive and most people had stained, painted or linoleum floors. Imitation tiles or parquet flooring were favourite patterns for halls and living rooms, whereas a dining room might be graced with a linoleum patterned to look like a Turkish carpet. Bedrooms were rarely carpeted, except with 'slip mats', but were often floored with flowered linoleum. In the 1930s Modernist patterns appeared on lino, in keeping with the wallpapers of the period. Linoleum was widely used in Australia, as in Britain, throughout the interwar years, especially in kitchens and bathrooms.

Where rooms were 'close covered', that is, with a fitted carpet, a rug was often laid on top. The two might match or contrast, as in a 1930s living room in which a handmade rug was combined with a fine Wilton carpet. Oriental carpets and rugs remained popular.

Rug designs – not only the patterns but also the shapes – might be tailored to the rooms. A rectangular rug with a semicircular extension at each end, for example, was

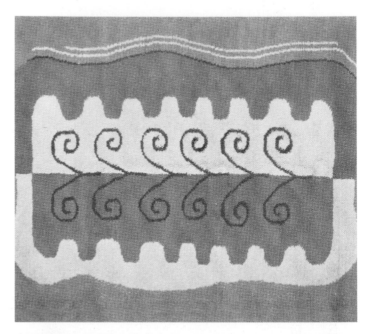

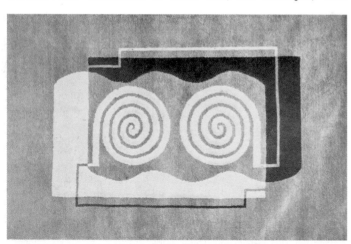

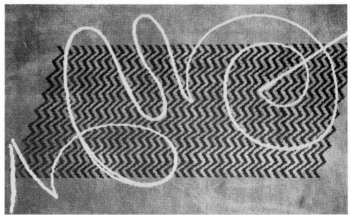

THIS PAGE AND OPPOSITE, BELOW: *Although in Victorian times rugs were a means of concealing or preventing wear in the carpet beneath, in the 1920s and 1930s they became an integral part of the room, with an aesthetic value far beyond the functional. The rugs were held to be 'a piece of concentrated expression, comparable perhaps to the actual title on the title-page of a book, which is also a thing designed as an indissoluble whole' (C. G. Tomrey).*

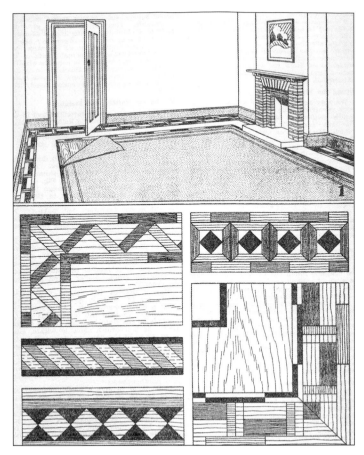

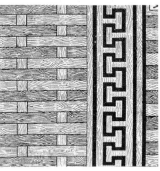

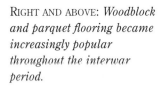

Right and above: *Woodblock and parquet flooring became increasingly popular throughout the interwar period.*

Left: *An illustration from a 'home handyman' book of the period, explaining how to imitate parquet inexpensively, using plywood coloured with wood stains.*

ETON · RURAL · FABRICS

LEFT: *Eton Rural Fabrics were destined for the kind of stylish modern interior suggested by this 1931 advertisement.*

OPPOSITE; *A selection of fabrics produced by Eton Rural Fabrics in the 1920s and early 1930s.*

recommended to make a long, narrow room look shorter and wider. Upper-class residences might sport a polar bearskin rug, along with lambskin for a bedcover.

Marion Dorn (1899–1964) was an important designer of carpets, as well as furnishing fabrics, during the 1930s. Nicknamed the 'architect of floors', she was an American who spent much of her working life in Britain, where she won an unrivalled reputation for textiles and tufted, sculpted carpets in Modernist designs, many of them simple and relatively inexpensive. Having collaborated for a decade or so with the graphic designer Edward McKnight Kauffer (1890–1954), whom she married, she established her own company in 1934, specializing in custom-designed rugs. Her handmade carpet designs included one based on interlacing circles; another featured concentric diamonds.

Textiles and fabrics

Textile designs for the mass market, like the architecture of the period, were dominated by the familiar and traditional until well into the 1930s. In an age of steel and concrete and glass, house-builders still clung to old forms and theories as well as to the materials that imposed those forms and theories: they still thought in terms of bricks, stone and wood. Similarly, textile designers continued to produce patterns for boudoirs and drawing rooms.

The lag behind the times was more noticeable in Britain than elsewhere in Europe. Modernism in Britain (according to Holbrook Jackson in 1933) was 'eccentric and uncertain', and also derivative: 'Many of our modernist designs speak English with a foreign accent.' Designers suffered from the 'illusion that modern design is a German

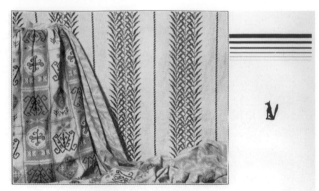

For QUALITY schemes
FOXTON FABRICS

Here is a group of woven fabrics in contemporary style from our large range which includes many fine examples of period and modern designs. From left to right: No. 4972 is one of our well-known Village Weaves and Nos. 5010 and 5017 are attractive woven fabrics, all produced in a number of good colours.

Awarded DIPLOMA d'HONNEUR and GOLD MEDALS PARIS - 1925 (EXPOSITION DES ARTS DECORATIFS) WHOLESALE ONLY

Obtainable at all leading Stores and Decorators

W · FOXTON · LTD
1 PATERNOSTER SQUARE and 1 & 2 ROSE STREET
LONDON, E.C.4
Telephone: CITY 2384 (3 lines)   Telegrams: SEARCHLIGHT, CENT, LONDON

Samples from the catalogues of makers of woven fabrics.

FAR LEFT: *British furnishing fabrics on display at the Paris International Exhibition 1938.*

LEFT: *Advertisement for Foxton Fabrics, who proudly announce gold medals and a Diploma d'Honneur won at the Paris Exposition in 1925.*

OPPOSITE, LEFT: *'Manhattan', a textile designed in block-printed cotton by Ruth Reeves.*

OPPOSITE, RIGHT: *A fine hand-tufted rug with animals in black and white on a lime-green ground, with foliage in brown, green and beige. The rug, designed by Nicholas de Moas, was put into production by Wilton Royal Carpet Co.*

or French export composed of cubes and triangles', inspired by a 'profound misunderstanding of the early cubist efforts of Picasso and his imitators'.

A modern furnishing textile could be any fabric that served the purpose of the designer. Materials that at one time had been taboo except for utility use, such as oil-cloth (or American cloth), were now elevated from the kitchen table to living-room lintels or windows. American cloth became very fashionable in the 1930s in Britain, and certain colours appeared more brilliant in this material than in any other. It was recognized to have limited use, however, and apparently it had an unpleasant smell.

Modernity also took the form of synthetic fabrics, which were being devised to meet new needs. At that time, these new fabrics were designated 'leather substitutes' or 'artificial silk', though the time would come when manufacturers and designers would combine to create original textures rather than copies of traditional materials. Meanwhile, durability was falling from favour, as buyers began to prefer a deliberate ephemerality, a conscious pursuit of variation.

In Britain, the artists Paul Nash and Duncan Grant produced pastel-coloured textiles that directly rejected the dark, sensuous shades of Art Nouveau. The husband-and-wife team of Edward McKnight Kauffer and Marion Dorn produced typically geometric and rectilinear Art Deco work. In France the textile industry revived in the 1930s, partly thanks to commissions for the liners *Ile de France* and *Normandie*, and partly to the involvement of the greatest artists, including Pablo Picasso, Henri Matisse and Raoul Dufy, whose painted designs were faithfully copied by tapestry weavers. The painter Charles Dufresne had brought the Art Deco style to tapestry. For the 1925 Exposition he depicted the story of 'Paul et Virginie' in tapestry that was used to upholster a suite of gilt-wood furniture, which Süe et Mare displayed in their pavilion, the Musée d'Art Contemporain.

The weaving workshop of the Bauhaus was a commercially successful venture. Its weavings often showed the influence of Paul Klee and were abstract in design. Gunta Stadler-Stölzl, Anni Albers and Lilly Reich, in turn heads of the weaving workshop, were talented designers themselves. Gunta Stadler-Stölzl (1897–1983) singlehandedly oversaw the Bauhaus weaving workshop from 1926 to 1931. It was thanks to her efforts and skill that mass production of Bauhaus textiles became a reality. She and two others from the Bauhaus set up a textile studio in Zurich, Switzerland. They produced commercial furnishing fabrics, notably geometric patterned rugs. The designs were put into production principally by Poly-textil Gesellschaft of Berlin and Pausa of Stuttgart.

Sonia Delaunay (1885–1979) was born in what is now the Ukraine. She was a pioneer abstract painter better known for her textile and fashion designs. After her marriage to the painter Robert Delaunay she created bold, abstract, geometric patterns and bright colours. She worked in textile designs from 1917, and also exhibited ceramics in Spain in 1919 and 1920.

Enid Marx (1902–93) was a British designer of wallpapers and fabrics. She is best known as the designer of seat upholstery for trains on the London Underground in

the 1930s. Ruth Reeves (1892–1966) studied in Paris between 1922 and 1928 and then returned to her native America, where she became known as a painter and designer of textiles and wallpapers. She worked in many different types of fabric, including chintz, voile, velvet and satin, and created a repeating abstract design for the carpets in Radio City Music Hall, New York.

A taste for the exotic and the brightly colourful characterized the textiles of the 1920s, emulating those seen in the Ballets Russes, the designs of William Morris of the Arts and Crafts Movement, and the art and artefacts of China, Japan, India and Egypt. As the years went on, however, there was a return to much more subdued colours such as brown, dull red, maroon and Brunswick green, while geometrical shapes derived from the work of Picasso and Léger infused the textiles of the 1920s and 1930s.

For furnishing fabrics, bedcovers and curtains, linens, velvets, tweeds, damasks, cottons, artificial silk taffetas, wool reps, crêpe-de-chine and oil-cloths were available. Tweeds came in chevron patterns; in other fabrics, geometrical and floral designs predominated. The fabrics could be smooth or gauged (textured). For curtains in a dining room of around 1937, the designer Duncan Miller

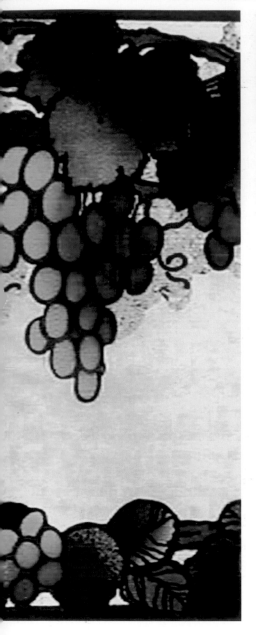

chose flame-coloured faced cloth. Liberty's of London brought out a new printed artificial silk velvet. This was a lustrous, strong fabric, enhanced by being crushed contrary to the pile at various points, thus giving pleasing effects of light and shade. Chair covers were generally made of cretonnes and chintzes, often in patterns that matched wallpaper designs.

Oil-silk, a rubberized product, was a dust-resistant, waterproof curtain material that could be sewn by hand or machine like any other fabric, but never faded or cracked nor needed washing. An all-silk material that wore well was shantung. Another luxury fabric was marabou (a fine raw silk), used for bedspreads and cushion covers. In wealthy homes, quilted satin was favoured for bedspreads, chair coverings, dressing-table hangings, cushion covers and even occasionally for walls. Synthetic fur provided a similarly opulent effect. Ox-hide was acceptable as an upholstery fabric.

Damask and Irish handkerchief linens adorned the fashionable dining table. Some tablecloths were embroidered or had a lace insert.

THIS PAGE AND OPPOSITE Floral and geometric designs were much loved for wallpapers and borders. The floral patterns were quite stylized and simpler and less intricate than the convoluted designs of Art Nouveau.

Wall finishes

Interior designers stressed the need to consider rooms as a complete entity and to give priority to harmony and aesthetics as much as to practical considerations such as durability and ease of cleaning. Woodwork, for example, should be considered in conjunction with the walls and could often be painted to match, diminishing the contrast between the surfaces and thus making the room seem bigger. When contrast was chosen, mahogany was thought to stand out well against shades of grey and to combine well and less starkly with creams or peachy pinks. For

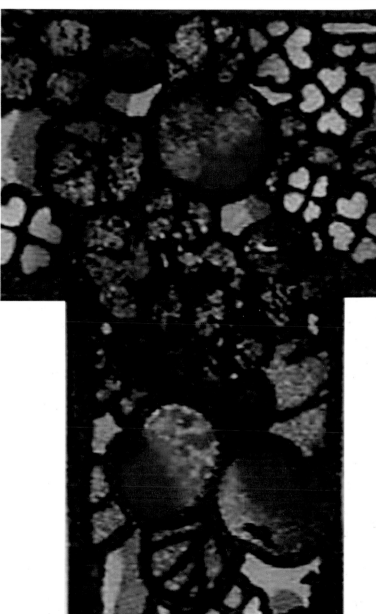

contrast, green went well with walnut, while a parchment (off-white) colour or a soft warm grey blended with it more quietly. Oak harmonized with pale yellow and was thrown into relief by blue, rose or wine-red; pure yellow and orange were less good with it.

In suburban houses in which the internal doors had not been wood-grained, it was a common practice to paint them in two colours. The frame would be painted in one colour and the panels in another. Popular pairings included red and yellow, brown and yellow and cream and green.

Paint was available for walls and ceilings in a wide range of soft colours and textures. Oil-based paint dried perfectly flat and hard, could be washed and was durable enough to last for years. It came in matt and gloss finishes. A compromise between the two was eggshell gloss, which was ideal for delicate colours and had the lively quality of a gloss paint but without its glare. Enamels were also used to achieve mirror-smooth, ultra-tough surfaces.

In the 1920s and 1930s, in the absence of standard paint shades, most professional house-painters in Britain mixed their own colours. There was a great difference in the lasting quality of good and bad (or cheap) paint at that time and house owners were of course advised never to choose the bad, which was simply a waste of the labour that applied it. When coloured paints were used, it was economical to varnish them, as this would stop them from fading. Water-based paints were also available, providing light or pastel effects. Aqualine was the trade name for ready-mixed distemper, or water paint, made by Mander Bros in the UK. Distemper was available in an enormous variety of very fine colours, which is perhaps why it remained very popular in the 1920s and 1930s. Painted floors were coming into favour in the 1930s: floor paints naturally needed to be durable. Grey and blue were popular.

Gloss paints were suitable for bathrooms and kitchens, as they resisted steam and were easy to clean. Special paints that gave a tile-like gloss and protection to the surface were available for spaces where steam and heat prevailed. They were inexpensive and came in a range of colours. A product called Celotex, an insulating cane fibre made in the USA, could be applied to walls and ceilings specifically to protect interiors from rapid changes in temperature and to guard against rot and fungal growth.

For dark rooms, highly glossy surfaces were appropriate, although such surfaces needed to be very

RIGHT AND OPPOSITE: Walls could be covered with paint or distemper or with wallpapers in more or less lavish patterns.

even or they would pick up irritating reflections. A stout underpaper or canvas could be applied to the wall before painting to improve matters. Ceilings were best painted in light, bright colours, but not with a gloss finish. A shining gold ceiling, of course, could look superb in some settings, but was hardly cheap as the effect could not be achieved with paint. Instead it had to be leaf of aluminium, lacquered gold or plain gold.

Stippled paint looked good, even under close examination, on a wall subject to glare. Other paint treatments that came into use in the early 1930s were combing and scumbling. Pleasing effects could be achieved by applying one colour over another. This did not work happily with distemper, which was the choice of the householder who could not afford oil-based paint, but the surface of the wet distemper could be stippled to ensure that it had no brush marks.

Duncan Miller, who designed domestic interiors, created a daring scheme for a bedroom with black walls in his Contemporary House, shown at London's Ideal Home

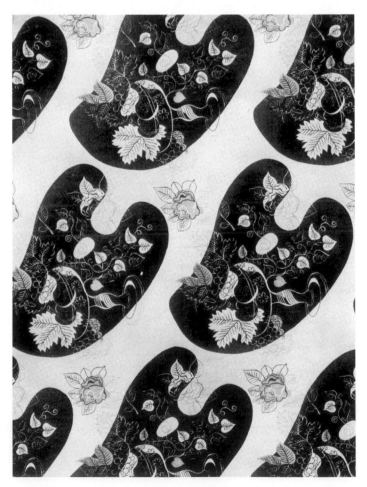

Exhibition in 1934. This gave a somnolent effect but, at the same time, suggested a filmstar's room for entertaining 'at home' rather than a conventional place for sleeping. It opened up boundless possibilities for contrast with white furnishings, white ceiling and coloured flower arrangements. A similarly bold scheme consisted of silver walls, matt grey paintwork and a shiny white ceiling, all set off by rich dark blue curtains lined with yellow. In the Salon des Artistes Décorateurs at the Paris International Exposition of 1937, A. Porteneuve exhibited a salon with walls of shiny black lacquer and an illuminated ceiling. The decorative elements within the room were white, black, green and natural leather.

Wallpapers

The most popular wallpapers were in geometric or tartan patterns, featuring rectangles of different sizes, checks, cross-hatching and triangles. Flower-posy motifs and marble, cloud or wave patterns were also fashionable. Bold outlines and strong colours were favoured, especially reds, golds, browns and 'fawn' (beige) for living rooms, where they were thought to go well with furniture painted in green or of natural wood or steel. Different wallpapers were often combined in the same room – for example, a bold-patterned paper behind the bed and on the ceiling of a bedroom, softened by a plainer paper around the remaining walls. The colours in the primary paper would be picked up in the plain paper and the border, as well as in the furnishings of the room, such as the carpet, rug, bedspread, chair covers and curtains.

Exotic wallpapers were fashionable in the 1920s: Chinese-lacquer imitations, desert scenes, Egyptian motifs, all-over leaf and berry patterns were available, with scenes from the Mediterranean and other landscapes as friezes. Preferred colours were quite loud – bright reds, blues and greens. Papers of the 1930s came in more muted colours such as soft greys, pinks and blues, but also in the so-called 'autumn tints' of oranges, browns, reds and greens.

Cheaper wallpapers were usually machine-printed with distemper on paper. Among the more expensive wallpapers were embossed examples with applied cut-out borders and corners, which were very popular in suburban houses in the 1930s; although at the very top end of the range homeowners thought such obvious decoration in bad taste and preferred to treat their walls with plain distemper. Besides ordinary wallpapers, various kinds of canvas and grass cloth (gold-or metallic-backed) were available.

By the mid-1930s scenic and flock wallpapers had gone out of fashion, as had decorative paper features such as friezes, cornices, ceiling borders and papers specially printed to make rococo panels. Nothing worthwhile had

come to take their place, according to the writer and designer Basil Ionides. In his book *Colour in Everyday Rooms* (1934), he condemned contemporary wallpaper designs as 'deplorable', adding:

> The good old designs were well drawn, and, though now old-fashioned, are still good. The modern designs, with few exceptions, are imitative and frankly bad, being produced purely commercially, with no real sense of quality and with almost total absence of good drawing.

Contrast was sought after: if the borders were elaborate, the wallpaper was probably plain, in a beige or cream colour and often embossed to give an interesting texture. There was usually a picture rail in all the downstairs rooms and there might also be a dado (or chair) rail in the hall and dining room. A relief paper, such as anaglytpa, might be hung below the dado rail, brush-grained and varnished to match the woodwork. In areas where a lot of wear could be expected, for example in halls and dining rooms, varnished papers were used. Over time, these took on a dark brown colour that smothered the original colour and pattern.

In the California bungalow and Spanish Mission houses of Australia, wallpapers were similar to those used in Britain. Homeowners happily papered their houses with lively 'Jazz Modern' wallpapers. British manufacturers thus retained a firm grip on Australia's wallpaper market. The most popular option was to combine a plain or textured filling paper in a neutral colour such as stone or cream with a brightly coloured cut-out border in a geometric design. In the 1930s, again following the British trend, householders chose more subdued colours, including the famous 'autumn tints' of reds, greens, yellows and browns, for wallpapers as well as carpets and furnishing textiles. Robin Boyd noted in *Australia's Home* (1952) that a typical home of the 1930s would have Jazz Modern wallpaper borders along with a cocktail cabinet of Queensland walnut, massive armchairs upholstered in Genoese velvet and a fitted Wilton carpet in a heavily patterned Modernist design.

OPPOSITE: *Windows of the interwar period often display beautiful designs and colours.*

THIS PAGE: *Intertwined initials, sunbursts, swags, wreaths and bouquets, as well as geometrical patterns were all popular for windows – as illustrated here by this page from a manufacturer's catalogue of 1928.*

Windows

In suburban houses windows were usually covered with frilled valances and light casement curtains of cotton, silk or rayon. 'Rufflette' tape was a novelty in the 1930s. It made simple work of curtain headings and it ensured even spacing of folds and a neat overall finish. Pelmet boards could be designed to look like a bay forming part of the ceiling, concealing the top of the curtains, which therefore made a dramatic impact, appearing to fall from nowhere.

Short screen curtains, placed low in the window and hung from rods and rings, were best made from artificial silk or rayon or from real linen or cotton. Muslin, lace or net curtains had to some extent gone out of fashion as they were difficult to keep clean. However, they continued to be used in some houses. Rayon was the best fabric. Taste had to be exercised: some people chose very violent colours for their net curtains, others, fussy objects that were indistinguishable from lingerie.

Roller blinds were available painted in designs such as Regency feathers. Venetian blinds in different colours, perhaps the tops of the slats contrasting with the undersides, gave pleasing results. The blinds could be made to run in a groove so that they would not flap, but this was a luxury add-on. Venetian blinds of American design were available in Britain. They were made of thin sheets of aluminium and had patent operating gear. Other blinds included those made of split laths or cane woven with cotton, which were usually stained green. Then there were linen blinds, which could be enlivened with pricked or printed patterns or even pictorial designs.

Old-fashioned jalousies (slatted shutters) were still to be found on many houses, but were often neglected by their owners who had allowed them to become stuck. Canvas striped blinds, now available in many colourways other than the original green-and-white or red-and-white, altered the angle at which light appeared to enter the room.

Ventilation was beginning to be considered actively, based on the principles of a properly arranged and balanced heating system, adequate provision for the exchange of air and an abundance of windows 'to give the sun a chance'.

The Lunken Window Company of Cincinnati, Ohio, offered the 'unit-window', a completely self-contained, ready-assembled unit, delivered with sash-cord, sash-

weights and fly-screens all in place. All the buyer had to do was to set the unit-window into the window opening of a building and apply plaster, trim and finish. The entire window could be used, with fly-screening, for ventilation in the summer. In the winter, weather-stripping bars ensured effective insulation. Metal weather strips sealed the cracks between sash and frame, promising to standardize the indoor temperature of the house with a concomitant saving of 20–40 per cent in coal consumption.

'Vita' glass windows offered rich, abundant, health-giving light (according to the advertisements), which admitted 'ultra-violet health rays', in contrast to ordinary window glass, which was alleged to 'dilute' light, just as skimmed milk is a pale substitute for full-cream milk.

Ground, sandblasted and acid-etched glass was now being produced in a range of modern patterns, and was again being used to 'obscure' windows where privacy was needed, such as in bathrooms and front doors, having been rejected in late Victorian times because of bad design.

Slightly bizarre, and well ahead of its time, was a house in Innsbruck, Austria, in which the vast window that formed one side of the living room could be lowered into the floor by means of an electric motor.

Lighting

Lamp design underwent a transformation soon after World War I when it was realized – first by Albert Simonet, of the firm of Simonet Frères – that electricity could not just be incorporated, with minor adaptations, into gas and candle fixtures, but that it required a whole new lighting aesthetic. Accordingly, the firm reduced its production of bronze and turned instead to the design of glass elements for lighting fixtures. A sculptor was commissioned to design sections of pressed translucent glass that would reflect light effectively from their surfaces.

Standard and table lamps were very common in 1920s and 1930s homes. The bases or brackets might be made of crystal, lacquer, wood, glass, brass, pewter, iron or other metal, pottery, alabaster or porcelain. The shades could be made of etched or tinted glass, paper, parchment, silk, satin, crinkle taffeta, muslin, canvas or worsted yarn. The designer Hayes Marshall went further – in one scheme he converted a canister into a lamp stand.

Concealed lighting, wall lamps and chandeliers were all considered in good taste. The new tubular lights were inset into some dressing tables and were beginning to prove useful for lighting hitherto inaccessible places: thus a

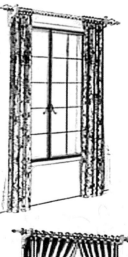

THIS PAGE AND OPPOSITE:
Pelmet boards, curtain rails and hooks and tracks.

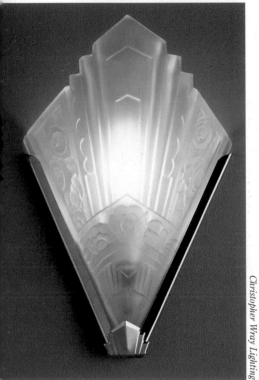

THIS PAGE AND OPPOSITE: *Many beautiful Art Deco light fittings are reproduced today and are understandably still popular.*

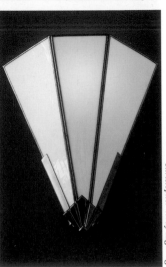

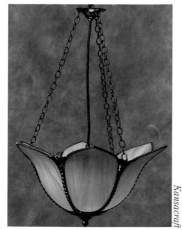

Kansacraft

Kansacraft

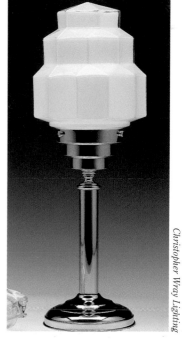

Christopher Wray Lighting

Christopher Wray Lighting

Rejuvenation Lamp & Fixture Co

Rejuvenation Lamp & Fixture Co

Kansacraft

Kansacraft

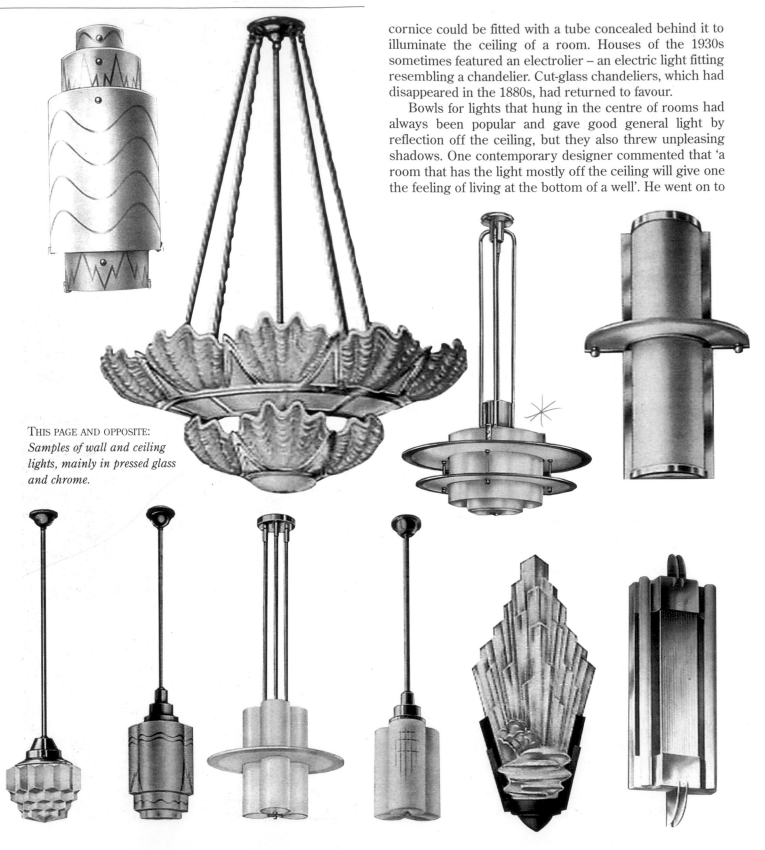

cornice could be fitted with a tube concealed behind it to illuminate the ceiling of a room. Houses of the 1930s sometimes featured an electrolier – an electric light fitting resembling a chandelier. Cut-glass chandeliers, which had disappeared in the 1880s, had returned to favour.

Bowls for lights that hung in the centre of rooms had always been popular and gave good general light by reflection off the ceiling, but they also threw unpleasing shadows. One contemporary designer commented that 'a room that has the light mostly off the ceiling will give one the feeling of living at the bottom of a well'. He went on to

THIS PAGE AND OPPOSITE:
Samples of wall and ceiling lights, mainly in pressed glass and chrome.

observe that dressing table lights in a bedroom should not be too flattering, 'as it is better to look one's best outside one's bedroom than in it' – a questionable assertion.

The Anglepoise lamp was invented in 1933 by George Carwardine, a British automobile engineer. The operation of the hinges in the lamp mimics the joints in a human arm. The flexibility and stability of the Anglepoise have made it the most popular desk lamp ever since, favoured particularly for office use.

Neon gas had been discovered in 1898. Enclosed in glass tubes and bombarded by electricity to create glowing colours for decorative effect, it became the now familiar neon lighting, but this did not happen until 1919, and it did not appear in the USA until 1923. Many of its present stylistic conventions are attributable to the Art Deco period. Neon signs were first added to older buildings to make them look modern, but by the 1930s neon was being used as an integral part of the concept of a building.

Gadgets

As more and more homes were connected to mains electicity during the 1920s and 1930s, a host of new electrical gadgets became available and were eagerly snapped up by the newly servantless households.

The electric iron became hugely popular, replacing the flat-iron, which needed constant reheating on the hob. By 1939, 77 per cent of households wired for electricity owned an electric iron.

Electrical toaster stoves and table waffle irons, the size of a modern sandwich toaster, could be bought from the 1910s in the USA, as could electric boilers, table stoves or grills, water kettles (in nickel plate or copper) and percolators. The Toast-O-Lator was an innovative toaster invented in the mid-1930s. It was chrome-plated, with a Bakelite base. The bread was grilled as it travelled from one side of the machine to the other on a miniature conveyor belt.

An electric chafing dish and cooker that cooked on the plate could make 'even a maidless Saturday night an occasion for entertaining'. Electric waffle irons were a novelty recently imported to Britain from the USA. Electric teapots and coffee percolators were also new aids to the hostess of the 1930s.

New in 1934 was the teamaker, the teaset on a tray with an electric alarm clock ingeniously connected to an electric kettle. When the alarm went off, the current under the kettle was switched on and the boiling water was then automatically poured into the teapot.

In line with the new fashion for sun-tans, sun lamps became available, which produced ultra-violet light and

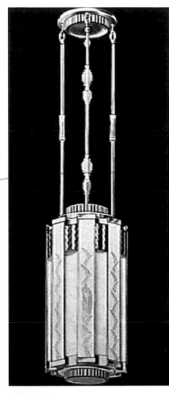

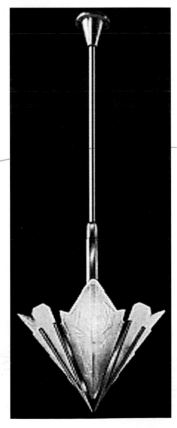
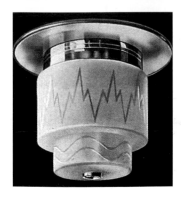

could be connected to any lighting or power point. Also on the market was the Mazda lamp with 'the wonderful non-sag filament' that prevented wastage of current.

A US magazine published in the year after World War I proudly blazoned the notion of 'electrocution' – what we would now, rather less alarmingly, call 'electrification' – in the laundry. The modern electrical time- and labour-saving devices included washers, dryers and 'ironers'.

The oscillating washer had a motor that swung the container to and fro. The bottom was corrugated or otherwise shaped to offer resistance and cause the friction that cleaned the clothes. The container was made of solid copper lined with planished (flattened and polished) tin to prevent corrosion. The washer could be permanently connected to a tub. Alternatives included the rotary or cylinder washer, in which the washing was put into a perforated cylinder, which revolved through the soapy water; and the vacuum washer, in which vacuum or suction cups rose and fell, drawing the water through the wash; and the 'dolly', in which clothes were washed in a semi-rotating device that looked like a milking stool.

Wringers on such machines could be stationary, swinging or sliding. Separate wringers, or mangles, existed in most households from the beginning of the twentieth century. They were used to squeeze water out of wet laundry and to smooth linen. They came in various forms and could be free-standing or mounted on a table.

The Ideal dryer consisted of units heated by gas, electricity or coal (if connected to a coal stove, when it received overflow heat). Inside it were a number of extendable racks. The motorized 'ironer' came in the form of a roller for flat pieces; unlike the mangle, which only folded items, the ironer was heated to give gloss and finish. All these machines were still expensive and unsophisticated in design and many housewives sent their washing out to laundries or local washerwomen.

Apart from electric irons, vacuum cleaners were the only electrical labour-saving appliances widely used in the years immediately after World War I. The cylindrical vacuum cleaner was introduced by Electrolux in 1915. It had a horizontal cylinder with a flexible hose to which brushes could be attached. In the USA, the American Hoover Suction Sweeper Company introduced an upright vacuum cleaner in 1916. It became the standard type for the next twenty years. The Hoover 700, made in 1920, had a

LEFT: *The harsh realities of war put an end to the flowing romanticism of Art Nouveau. The straight lines and functional forms of Art Deco make a sharp contrast.*

*An electric
toaster stove for
heating milk or
water or for
griddle cakes
and, with a grill,
for toasting,
comes at $9.50*

*No grease is
necessary for this
electric table
waffle iron.
Cooks two waf-
fles 3½" square
in a minute and
a half. Nickel
plated, $15*

LEFT AND BELOW : *Appliances
and gadgets for the home, then
as now, were made in many
different forms and styles, to
suit different functions, tastes,
budgets and degrees of luxury.*

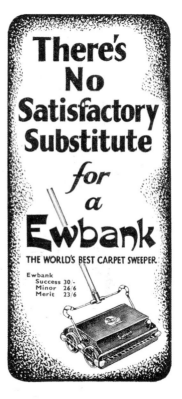

canvas bag in which was stowed a disposable paper sack for collecting the dust. Like modern models, it featured rotating brushes that loosened the dust, which was then sucked into the cleaner. The brushes, fan and motor were all housed in a single casing. The head was adjustable.

Goblin, the brand name of the British Vacuum Cleaner and Engineering Co., who claimed to be 'the originators of vacuum cleaning', now aimed to 'simplify' the ownership of a vacuum cleaner for 'thousands of women', by offering moderate cost, amazing suction power and extreme simplicity. Vac-Tric, a firm based in Cricklewood, London,

also claimed to have produced the first all-British electric vacuum cleaners. They were cylinder cleaners, with cylinders made of steel with a crocodile-leather-finish.

Vacuum cleaners came with various attachments for floors and upholstery and a polishing brush for parquet and linoleum. In some cleaners, the dustbag ran on rubber-tyred wheels. By the 1930s, the vacuum cleaner was much used and the electric floor polisher was also finding its way into householders' affections, especially if it had a large triangular brush suitable for polishing large surfaces.

Stockists

The lists of stockists given on these pages cannot be exhaustive and are intended only as a starting and commercial telephone directories are always worth looking at and are good sources of information about your own area. Alternatively, there are many organisations giving specialist information and advice and those who will search for specific item. The internet is another area worth exploring.

United Kingdom

The Museum of Domestic Design & Architecture (MoDA) has a permanent exhibition showing how we inhabited our homes from 1900 to 1960.
MoDA, Middlesex University
Cat Hill Barnet
Hertfordshire
EN4 8HT
Tel: 020 8411 5244
www.moda@mdx.ac.uk

Accessories

Deco & Decorative
104 Greenwich South Street
London SE10 8UM
Tel: 0208 692 4808

Decomania
9 College Approach
London SE10 9HY
Tel: 0208 858 8180

Déjà Vu Antiques
23 Grosvenor Street
Chester
CH1 2DD
Tel: 01233 315625

Flying Duck Enterprises
320-322 Creek Road
London SE10 9SW
Tel: 0208 858 1964

Radio Days
87 Lower Marsh Street
London SE1 7AB
Tel: 0207 928 0800

Reminis
Gledrid Industrial Park
Chirk
Wrexham
LL14 5DG
Tel: 01691 778899

20th Century Marks
12 Market Square
Westerham
Kent TN16 1AW
Tel: 01959 5622221

Retro City
39 High Street Antiques Centre
Hastings
East Sussex TN34 3EN
Tel: 01424 460068

Architectural Salvage

Brondesbury Architectural
  Reclamation
The Yard, 136 Willesden Lane
London NW6 7TE
Tel: 0207 328 0820

Dorset Reclamation
The Reclamation Yard
Bere Regis
Dorset BH20 7JZ
Tel: 01929 472200

Drummonds Artichectural Antiques Ltd
The Kirkpatrick Buildings
25 London Road, Hindhead
Surrey GU26 6SB
Tel: 01428 609444

Grate Fireplaces & Interiors
79 North Street
Portslade
Sussex BN41 1DH
Tel: 01273 416679
www.gratefireplaces.co.uk

The Original Architectural
  Salvage Co Ltd
South Gloucester Street
Dublin 2
Tel: 00 353 86 8207700
www.arcsalve.ie

Solopark plc
Station Road, Pampisford
Cambridgeshire CB2 4HB
Tel: 01223 834663
www.solopark.co.uk

Walcot Reclamation
108 Walcot Street
Bath BA1 5BG
Tel: 01225 444404

Welsh Salvage Company
ISCA Yard, Milman Street
Newport
South Wales NP9 2LG
Tel: 01633 212945

Bathrooms

Aston Matthews
141-147A Essex Road
Islington
London N1 2SN
Tel: 0207 354 5951

Catchpole & Rye, Posh Tubs
Moriati's Workshop
High Halden,
Ashford
Kent TN26 3LZ
Tel: 01233 850155

Colourwash Bathrooms
1 Broomhall Buildings
Sunningdale
Berkshire SL5 0DH
Tel: 01344 872096

Heritage Bathrooms
Princell Street
Bedminster
Bristol BS3 4AG
Tel: 0117 953 5000

Imperial Towel Rails Ltd
Jupiter House
Orbital Way
Cannock
Staffordshire WS11 3XW
Tel: 01543 571615
www.imperialtowelrails.com

Miscellanea
Crossways
Churt
Farnham, Surrey
Tel: 01428 714014

Shires
Beckside Road
Bradford
West Yorkshire BD7 2JE
Tel: 01274 521199

Thomas Crapper & Co Ltd
The Stable Yard
Alscot Park
Stratford-on-Avon
Warwickshire CV37 8BL
Tel: 01789 450 522

The Water Monopoly
16/18 Lonsdale Road
London NW6 6RD
Tel: 0207 624 2636

Doors & Windows
Bradbury's Stained Glass
34 High Street
Barnet EN5 5RU
Tel: 0208 449 2563

The Designer Door Company
Bow Wharf
Grove Road
London E3 5SN
Tel: 0208 880 6739

GBS Joinery
Mill Street
Hazel Grove
Stockport
Cheshire SK7 4AR
Tel: 0161 456 0501

Peco of Hampton
72 Station Road, Hampton
Middlesex TW12 2BT
Tel: 0208 979 8310

Traditional Joinery & Furniture
Lower Knapp Green
Little Dewchurch
Hereford HR2 6PP
Tel: 01432 840600

Fireplaces
Architectural Antiques
70 Pembroke Street
Bedford MK40 3RQ
Tel: 01234 213131

Old Flames
30 Long Street
Easingwold
York YO6 3HT
Tel: 01347 821188

Olde Englande Reproductions
Unit 7 & 9
Lonpark Industrial Estate,
Chadwick Street
Longton
Stoke-on-Trent ST3 1JP
Tel: 01782 319350
www.oldenglande.fsnet.co.uk

Olde Worlde Fireplaces
118 Blandford Square
Newcastle-upon-Tyne
Tel: 0191 261 9229

Flooring & Rugs
Attica
543 Battersea Park Road
London SW11 3BL
Tel: 0207 738 1234

Fired Earth
Twyford Mill
Oxford Road
Adderbury
Oxfordshire OX17 3HP
Tel: 01295 814300

Kirkstone
128 Walham Green Court,
Moore Park Road
London SW6 4DG
Tel: 0207 381 0424

The Rug Centre Ltd
68 Spith Street
Dorking
Surrey RH4 2HD
Tel: 01306 882202
also at
64 South Street, Exeter
Devon EX1 1EE
Tel: 01392 410151

Wellington Tile Company
Tone Estate, Milverton Road
Wellington
Somerset TA21 0AZ
Tel: 01823 667242

World's End Tiles
Silverthorne Road
Battersea
London SW8 3HE
Tel: 0207 819 2100

Furniture
Aero
347-349 King's Road
London SW3 5ES
Tel: 0207 351 0511

All in the Past
1063 London Road
Leigh-on-Sea
Essex SS9 3JP
Tel: 01702 713101

Lutyens Design Associates
61 St John's Avenue
London SW15 6AL
Tel 0208 780 5977

Amazing Emporium
249 Cricklewood Broadwood
Broadway
London NW2 6NX
Tel: 0208 208 1616/0704

Bed Bazaar
The Old Station
Station Road
Framlingham
Suffolk IP13 9EE
Tel: 01728 723756

The Conran Shop
Michelin House
81 Fulham Road
London SW3 6RD
Tel: 0207 589 7401

R & D Davidson
Romsey House
51 Maltravers Street
Arundel
West Sussex BN18 9BQ
Tel: 01903 883 141

Restall Brown & Clennell Ltd
120 Queensbridge Road
London E2 8PD
Tel: 0207 739 6626

Kitchens
Crabtree Kitchens
The Twickenham Centre
Norcutt Road
Twickenham TW2 6SR
Tel: 0208 755 1121

Fulham Kitchens
19 Carnwath Road
London SW6 3HR
Tel: 0207 736 6458

Greenwich Woodworks
1 Friendly Place
Lewisham Road
London SE13 7QS
Tel: 0208 694 8449

Trevor Moore Designs Ltd
The Design Gallery
7 Weavers Walk
Newbury
Berkshire RG14 1AL
Tel: 01635 523990
www.scoot.co.uk/trevor_moore

The Utility Room
PO Box 3436
Wareham
Dorset BH20 4YP
Tel: 10929 471327

Lighting
Angelo's
131-137 Turnpike Lane
London N8 0DU
Tel: 0208 348 5460

Christopher Wray Lighting
591/593 King's Road
London SW6 2YW
Tel: 0207 736 8434

Hector Finch
88-90 Wandsworth Bridge Road
London SW6 2TF
Tel: 0207 731 8886
www.hectorfinch. com

Fritz Fryer
12 Brookend Street
Ross-on-Wye
Herefordshire HR9 7EG
Tel: 01989 567416

Kansa Kraft
The Flour Mill
Wath Road
Elsecar
Barnsley
South Yorkshire S74 8HW
Tel: 01226 747424

Lights on Broadway
Unit 10A 98
Victoria Road
London NW10 6NB
Tel: 0208 453 1656

Magic Lanterns at By George
23 George Street
St Albans
Herts AL3 4ES
Tel: 01727 865680/853032

Two Zero C Applied Art
56 Abbey Business Centre
Ingate Place
London SW8 3NS
Tel: 0207 720 2021

Radiators & Ironwork
Beaumont Foundries
Lower Farm, Brandon Lane
Coventry CV3 3GW
Tel: 01203 511055

Faral Radiators
Tropical House
Charlwoods Road
East Grinstead
West Sussex RH19 2HJ
Tel: 01342 305420/317171

Hargreaves Foundry
Water Lane
South Parade
Halifax HX3 9HG
Tel: 01422 330607

Heating World Group Ltd
Excelsior Works
Eyre Street
Birmingham B18 7AD
Tel: 0232 454 2244

The Radiator Company
Elan House
Charlwoods Road
East Grinstead
West Sussex RH19 2HG
Tel: 01342 302250

Sinclair Classical Rainwater Systems
Sinclair Works
PO Box 3
Ketley
Telford TF1 4AD
Tel: 01952 262500

Radiating Style
Unit 15, Derby Road Industrial Estate
Derby Road, Hounslow
Middlesex TW3 3UQ
Tel: 0208 577 9111

USA
Architectural salvage
Architectural Artifacts
2207 Carimer Street
Denver
CO 80033
Tel: 303 292 6812

Architectural Salvage Inc
Brentwood
NH 03933
Tel: 603 642 4348
www.oldhousesalvage.com

Kimberley's Old House Gallery
1600 Jonquill Ln
Wausau
WI 54401
Tel: 715 359 5077

Off the Wall-Architectural Antiques
PO Box 4561
Third S E Lincoln and Fifth
Carmel
CA 93921
Tel: 831 624 6165
www.imperialearth.com/OTW/

Olde Good Things
124 W 24th Street
New York
NY 10011
Tel: 212 989 8401
www.oldegoodthings.com

The Old House Parts Co
24 Blue Wave Mall
Kennebunk
ME 04043
Tel: 207 985 1999
www.oldhouseparts.com

Pinch of the Past
109 W Broughton Street
Savannah
GA 31401
Tel: 912 232 5563

Architectural hardware
Al Bar Wilmette Platers
127 Green Bay Road
Wilmette Illinois 60091
Tel: 847 251 0187

American Home Supply
191 Lost Lake Lane
Campbell
CA 95008
Tel: 408 246 1962

Antique Hardware & Home Store
19 Buckingham Plantation Drive
Bluffton
SC 29910
Tel: 843 837 9796

Ball & Ball
463 W Lincoln Highway
Exton
PA 19341
Tel: 610 363 7330

Bona Decorative Hardware
3073 Madison Road
Cincinnati
OGH 45209
Tel: 513 321 7877

Classic Gutter Systems
8294 East Michigan
Galesburg, MI 49053
Tel: 616 382 2700
www.classicgutters.com

Crown City Hardware
1047 N Allen Avenue
Dept 01098
Pasadena, CA 91104
Tel: 626 794 0234
www.crowncityhardarw.com

Liz's Antique Hardware
453 S LaBrea Avenue
Los Angeles
CA 90036
Tel: 323 939 4403
www.lahardware.com

Nostalgic Warehouse
701 E Kingsley Road
Garland, TX 75041
Tel: 800 522 7336
www.nostalgicwarehouse.com

Renovators Old Mill
Dept 2467
Millers Falls
MA 01349
Tel: 800659 0203

The Roof Tile and Slate Co
1209 Carroll
Carrollton
Texas 75006
Tel: 800 446 0005

Van Dyke's Restorers
Dept 60179
PO Box 278
Woonsocket
SD 57385
Tel: 800 558 1234

Bathrooms
Affordable Antique Bath and More
333 Oak Street
PO Box 444
San Andreas
CA95249
Tel:209 754 1797

American Chine
6615 W Boston St
Chandler
AZ 85226
Tel: 800 359 3261

Baths from the Past
83 East Water Street
Rockland, MA 02370
Tel: 800 697 3871

Mac the Antique Plumber
6325 Elvas Avenue
Dept OHJ
Sacramento , CA 95819
Tel: 916 454 4507
www.antiqueplumber.com

Pierce Decorative Hardware &
  Plumbing
6823 Snider Plaza
Dallas , TX 75235
Tel: 214 368 2851

Renovators Old Mill\
Dept 2467
Millers Falls
MA 01349
Tel: 800659 0203

Shank & Nickell Kitchen & Bath
Works
736 Walnut Street
Royersford
PA 19468
Tel: 610 948 9200

Doors & Windows
Allied Window Inc
2724 W McMicken Avenue
Cincinnati
Ohil 45214
Tel: 800 445 4311

Amherst Woodworking & Supply
30 Industrial Drive
Northampton
MA 01061
Tel: 413 584 3003

Artistic Doors & Windows
10 S Inman Avenue
Avenel
NJ 07001
Tel: 908 726 9400

Authentic Stained Glass
12824 Hwy 431
Suite G
Guntersville
AL 35976
Tel: 205 582 7848

Beveled Glass Works
23852 Pacific Coast Hwy
Ste PMB351
Malibu, CA 90265
Tel: 310 457 5252

Burnham & LaRoche Associates
  Stained Glass
441 Fulton Street
Medford
MA 02155
Tel: 800 540 5047

Ciro C Coppa
1231 Paraiso Avenue
San Pedro
CA 90731
Tel: 310 548 4142

J F Day Co
2820 6th Avenue So
Birmingham
Alabama
Tel: 205 322 6776

Designer Doors Inc
Tel: 800 2341 0525
www.designerdoors.com
Marvin Windows & Doors
Tel: 800 268 7644
www.marvin.com

Peachtree Doors & Windows
PO Box 5700
Norcross
GA 30091
Tel: 800-PEACH99
www.peach99.com

Shuttercraft
282 Stepstone Hill
Guilford, CT 06437
Tel: 203 453 1973

Stained Glass Overlay
1827 North Case Street
Orange
CA 92865
Tel: 800 944 4746
www.sgoinc.com

Timberlane Woodcrafters Inc
197 Wissahickon Avenue
North Wales
PA 19454
Tel: 800 250 2221

Vixen Hill Shutters
OHJ9 Main Street
Elverson
PA 19520
Tel: 800 423 2766

Jack Wallis Stained Glass & Doors
2985 Butterworth Road
Murray
KY 42071
Tel: 502 489 2613

Fireplaces
ADI Corp
5000 Nicholson Ct
N Bethesda
MD 20895
Tel: 301 468 6856

Architectural Accents
2711 Piedmont Road
Atlanta
GA 30305
Tel: 404 266 8700

Authentic Stained Glass
12824 Hwy 431
Suite G
Guntersville
AL 35976
Tel: 205 582 7848

Draper & Co
2011 Stratford Rd S E
Decatur
AL 35601
Tel: 800 549 8846

Ellite Fireplace Facing
6540 Pflumm Road
Shawnee
KS 66216
Tel: 913 631 5443

Fires of Tradition
316 Brock Road
Greensville
ON L9H 5H5
Tel: 905 627 4147

Mantels of Yesteryear
70 W Tennessee Avenue
PO Box 908
McCaysville
GA 30555-0908
Tel: 706 492 5534
www.mantelsofyesteryear.com

Superior Fireplace
PO BOx 2066
4325 Artesia Avenue
Fullerton
CA 92833-2522
Tel: 714 521 7302

The Hearth Collection
1636 W 135th Street
Gardena, CA 90259
Tel: 310 323 6720
www.stonemfg.com

Kitchens
Classic Cookers
R D 3
Box 180
Montpelier, VT 05602
Tel: 802 223 3620

Crownpoint Cabinetry
153 Charleston Road
Claremont
NH 03743
Tel: 800 999 4994

Dacor
950 South Raymond Avenue
Pasadena, CA91109-7202
Tel: 800 772 7778

Exquisite Surfaces
731 North La Cienega Boulevard
Los Angeles
CA 90069
Tel: 310 659 4580

Good Time Stove Co
PO Box 306
Goshen, MA 01032
Tel: 413 268 3677
www.goodtimestove.com

Heritage Custom Kitchens
215 Diuller Avenue
New Holland
PA 17557
Tel: 717 354 4011

Mark Brady, Housewright
151 Westwood Ln
Middletown
CT 06457 1965
Tel: 860 346 9069
www.markbradyhousewright.com

The Original German Silver Sink Co
5754 Lodewyck
Detroit
MI 48224
Tel: 313 882 7730

Lighting
Alan's Custom Lighting Repair
1037 Taft Street
Rockville
MD 20850
Tel: 301 340 1058

American Home Supply
191 Lost Lake Lane
Campbell
CA 95008
Tel. 408 246 1962

American Period Lighting
3004 Colombia Avenue
Lancaster, PA 17603
Tel: 717 392 5649
www.americanperiod.com

Antique Lighting Co
1000 Lenora
Ste 314
Seattle
WA 98121
Tel: 206 622 8298

Century House Antique Lamp
Emporium & Repair
46785 Rt 18 W
Wellington OH 44090
Tel: 440 647 4092

Light Power
59A Wareham St
Boston
MA 02118
Tel: 617 423 9790

Metropolitan Lighting Fixture Co
200 Lexington Avenue
Showroom 512
New York NY 10016
Tel: 212 545 0032

Rejuvenation Lamp & Fixture Co
2550 N W Nicolai Street
Portland
Oregon 97210
Tel: 888 343 8548
www.rejuvenation.com

Gaslight Time
5 Plaza St W
Brooklyn
NY 11217
Tel: 718 789 7185

Renovators Old Mill
Dept 2467
Millers Falls
MA 01349
Tel: 800659 0203

Roy Electric Co Inc
22 Elm Street
Westfield
NJ 07090
Tel: 908 317 3347

Things Deco
130 E 18 Street, Suite 8F
New York
NY 10003
Tel: 212 362 8961

Urban Archaeology
143 Franklin Street
New York
NY 10013
Tel: 212 431 4646
www.homeportfolio.com

BIBLIOGRAPHY

V. Arwas, *Art Deco* (London, 1980/revised edn 1992)
Australia's Yesterdays: A look at our recent past, Sydney, Reader's Digest Services, 1934
Martin Battersby, *The Decorative Thirties*, London, 1988
Martin Battersby, *The Decorative Twenties*, London, 1969
Robin Boyd, *Australia's Home*, [Australia], 1952
British Wallpapers in Australia 1870-1940, Conservation Resource Centre of the Historic Houses Trust of New South Wales, 1995
Yvonne Brunhammer, *The Nineteen Twenties Style*, London, Cassell, 1969 (rev. 1987)
Yvonne Brunhammer and Suzanne Tise, *French Decorative Art, 1900-1942*, Paris, 1990
P. Cabanne, *Encyclopédie Art Déco*, Paris, 1986
Noel Carrington, *Design and a Changing Civilization*, London, 1935
Henry J. Cowan, *From Wattle and Daub to Concrete and Steel: the English Heritage of Australia's Buildings*, Melbourne, Melbourne University Press, 1998
M. Dufrene, ed., *Authentic Art Deco Interiors*, Woodbridge, Suffolk, 1990 [illustrates the ninety-six interiors in the 1925 Exposition in Paris]
Alastair Duncan, *American Art Deco*, London, 1986
Alastair Duncan, *Art Deco*, London, Thames and Hudson, 1988 (rev. 1997)
Alastair Duncan, *Art Deco Furniture: The French Designers*, London, 1984
Kenneth Frampton, *Modern Architecture*, London, Thames & Hudson, 1992
Philippe Garner, ed., *Phaidon Encyclopedia of Decorative Arts 1890-1940*, London and Oxford, Phaidon Press, 1978 (paperback, 1988)
John E. Gloag, *Artifex, of the Future of Craftsmanship*, London, 1926
John E. Gloag, *Industrial Art Explained*, London, 1934
William Hardy, Steven Adams and Arie van de Lemme, *The Encyclopedia of Decorative Styles 1850-1935*, London, New Burlington Books, 1988
Bevis Hillier, *Art Deco of the 20s and 30s*, London, 1968 (rev. 1985)

Guy Julier, *The Thames and Hudson Encyclopaedia of 20th Century Design and Designers*, London, Thames and Hudson, 1993
Dan Klein, *All Colour Book of Art Deco*, photographs by Angelo Hornak, London, Octopus Books, 1974
Osbert Lancaster, *Homes Sweet Homes*, London, 1939 (rev. 1953)
Alain Lesieutre, *The Spirit and Splendour of Art Deco*, London, 1974
Little Palaces: The Suburban House in North London, 1919-1939, An exhibition organised by Middlesex University and the Borough of Enfield's Community Programme, with funding from the Manpower Services Commission and the John Lewis Partnership, 1987
Nikolaus Pevsner, *An Enquiry into Industrial Art in England*, 1937
Anthony Quiney, *House and Home: A History of the Small English House*, London, BBC, 1976
Herbert Read, *Art and Industry*, London, 1934
J. M. Richards, *The National Trust Book of English Architecture*, London, National Trust and Weidenfeld & Nicolson, 1981
W. J. Splatt, *Architecture (The Arts in Australia)* [Australia]
Penny Sparke, *An Introduction to Design and Culture in the Twentieth Century*, London, Allen & Unwin, 1986
Judy Spours, *Art Deco Tableware: British Domestic Ceramics 1925-1939*, Ward Lock, 1988
Susan A. Sternau, *Art Deco*, New York, Todtri Productions, and London, Tiger Books International, 1997
Michael Tambini, *The Look of the Century*, London, Dorling Kindersley, 1996 (rev. 1998)
Jane Shoaf Turner, ed., *The Dictionary of Art*, London, Macmillan, 1996; entries including Art Deco, Walter Gropius, Le Corbusier, Mies van der Rohe, Modernism, Jacques-Emile Ruhlmann
W. Uecker, *Art Deco: Die Kunst der zwanziger Jahre*, Munich, 1984
David Watkin, *A History of Western Architecture*, London, Laurence King Publishing, 1986 (paperback 1992)